FOLLOWERSHIP

A PRACTICAL GUIDE TO

SURVIVING
LEADERS

GEOFFREY BOND

ISBN (Print): 978-1-09837-787-8
ISBN (eBook): 978-1-09837-788-5

To Mary Alice, Josh, and Nick.
Where would I be without your love and unwavering support?
I'd follow you anywhere.

Contents

Introduction

Followership. There are thousands, no, make that tens of thousands of books on the market at any given moment about leadership. Add to that the innumerable seminars, studies, scholarly articles, research projects, conferences, surveys, and so on. You'd think that leadership was the single most important issue facing humankind today - more important than cell phone network coverage, greater tasting light beer, and climate change. Combined.

But the truth is just the opposite. The world is not facing a leadership crisis. We've got plenty of leaders. Too many, in fact. Way too many. How many leaders does an organization really need? The answer, of course, is one. And how many leaders does an organization typically have? Research shows that the number of leaders in an organization is the product of the number of organizational members multiplied by the square root of one. For those of you who would rather not do the math here, the answer, not so coincidently, is that the number of leaders in any given organization is equal to the number of members of said organization.

Everybody's a leader today. Or an aspiring leader. Or a chief, supervisor, boss, director, head honcho, captain, manager, executive, chair, foreman... Nobody's a follower. Nobody. Not anymore.

And the irony of all this is that, in short, leadership is overrated. It gets too much credit and way too much blame. Most organizations have achieved their greatest successes in spite of their leaders- not because of them. It's all about the followers. It's always been all about the followers. And it's about time the world wakes up to it.

Congratulations to you. The fact that you have read even this far in a book about followership means that you are probably not a jerk. Followers represent some of the kindest, most compassionate, and best all-around people on the planet - like special educators, Mother Teresa, nursing home volunteers, and Tom Hanks all rolled into one. Followers are not driven by control, power, fame, fortune, or sex with interns. They've set aside their own personal glory for the greater good. It's not about them. It's about the organization, specifically furthering the organization's mission, which they support with all their heart and soul, even if it means making their idiot supervisor look competent from time to time.

An effective follower understands that her leader is a flawed human being, driven by ego and self-importance or the necessity to accept a promotion they're not ready for in order to pay off a divorce attorney from two marriages ago. While recognition and approval are nice, effective followers are there first and foremost to support a worthy mission, not an ego. Followership is a means- not an end. Effective followers do not surrender to some guru, lose their sense of self, or forget why they're following in the first place. Effective followers eclipse bad leaders.

This modest tome before you will define effective followership and explore its many facets. Regardless of whether you are just starting your career, midway up the corporate ladder, or the boss's nephew with a corner office and no real responsibilities, practicing the concepts presented in these pages will greatly improve your professional life. If you aspire to a leadership role, incorporating the pillars of effective followership into your work life will help you on your journey and, more importantly, help you be successful once you get there. Good followers make the best leaders.

Best of all, there isn't any sleight of hand presented here for you to practice. This is not some phony way of manipulating clients, coworkers, and bosses into changing their workplace perception of you. In fact, it's just the opposite. This book will help you experience profound changes in the way you perceive yourself. Any behavioral or attitudinal adjustments you make will flow naturally from this renaissance. These are not skills. They are principles and practices that will fundamentally change how you view your place in the cosmos, your work relationships and maybe even your personal ones.

Now let's do this!

CHAPTER 1:

Nazis, Teenagers, and Cults.
But Not Necessarily in That Order.

JOSEPH CAMPBELL: "Follow your bliss…"

ME: "Don't go chasing after your bliss. When you
do the right thing, your bliss follows *you*."

Before jumping into this discourse, I have to acknowledge the elephant in the room. Come on now. I know you're thinking it. If followership is so great, then how come it's gotten such a bad rap in all the organizational development literature and with parents and middle school guidance counselors the world over? The answer, in a nutshell, has to do with teens, cults, and Nazis. Seriously.

Let's start with teenagers. When a kid comes home from school and announces to Mom and Dad that he wants to join the debate team because all his friends are joining, they will invariably turn their attention from cable's highest rated news commentary program and respond with that Zen koan-like expression passed from generation to generation: "If all your friends jumped off a bridge would you?" Any kid will tell you, there is no right way to answer that. It's a stupid question. There may be a hundred excellent reasons to jump off a bridge with your friends or a hundred excellent reasons to join the debate team, a good one being to learn how to respond to these kinds of questions. There's nothing reasonable a kid can say here that won't result in the temporary confiscation of a smartphone. The damage has been done. The message from Mom and Dad is clear: "Following others is bad."

Parents are just flat out wrong here. Being a follower isn't necessarily a bad thing any more than being a leader is automatically good. Jumping off a bridge because all your friends jumped off, for better or for worse, is just the way it is. Judith Rich Harris, in her book, *The Nurture Assumption: Why Children Turn Out the Way They Do,* presents a convincing argument that a kid's peer group is more influential than his parents in his development. Well, duh. I've never met a kid yet, aside from my own, who wanted to be cool like his parents. Kids want to be cool like their friends. They want to dress like their friends, talk like their friends, jump from infrastructure like their friends. Parents (and school guidance personnel) should stop criticizing followership and accept it. It's a part of life. If parents don't like the results, they should get their kids a better class of friends. And let me know how that works out for you.

Cults, too, have contributed to the bad reputation of followership- and with good reason. Any organization that exists for the sole benefit of its leadership is a stinker. Bad followers, like those in cults and certain garden clubs, follow for all the wrong reasons. One of the biggest of which is to win the approval of the charismatic nut job who runs the joint. In fact, their *raison d'être* is to keep in their leaders' good graces, and they're willing to do just about anything to this end.

When bad leaders meet bad followers, the results can be disastrous. In 1997, thirty-nine members of the Heaven's Gate cult, including group leader Marshall Applewhite, committed suicide. Applewhite convinced them that upon death their souls would be transported to a spaceship that was following the Hale-Bopp comet, which was fast approaching Earth. The members ate applesauce laced with a heavy helping of phenobarbital, washed it down with a quart of vodka, and just to be on the safe side, tied plastic bags over their heads.

Their bodies were found lying neatly in bunk beds, each covered by a purple cloth. All were dressed in black shirts, black sweat pants, and new Nike cross trainers. Apparently, outer space does not have an EZ Pass lane, as each was carrying a five-dollar bill and some change for the toll. Really. It was later discovered that seven members of the group had voluntarily underwent castration in Mexico at the urging of Applewhite, which affirms the old adage of American politics, "When you've got 'em by the balls, their hearts and minds will follow." You'd think this would go without saying, but apparently not: If you find yourself in the examining room of a Tijuana urgent care facility, patiently waiting for your turn to be castrated, maybe, just maybe, things have gone too far.

Confirming the prescience of Godwin's law, I'd like to turn now to the Nazi portion of our program. Godwin's Law: In any online discussion, regardless of the topic, sooner or later someone somewhere somehow will compare someone or something to Adolf Hitler and the Nazis.

I think Indiana Jones in the movie *Indiana Jones and the Last Crusade* said it best, "Nazis. I hate these guys." Even Professor Jones couldn't have predicted the part they would play in how followership came into our collective consciousness as bad- really bad. Nazi bad. During World War II, the extent of the Nazi atrocities was not common knowledge among the U.S. populace. In 1942, when the U.S. State Department finally confirmed that two million Jews had already been murdered in Europe, the Washington Post put the story on page six; the New York Times had it on page ten. When the war finally ended, the good people of Earth needed a way to assuage their collective guilt for allowing horrible things to happen to far too many people for far too long. Enter the Nuremberg trials.

In 1945 and 1946, the winning side— the United States, Great Britain, France, and the Soviet Union —conducted military tribunals for twenty-two prominent Nazis in Nuremberg, Germany. Most of the defendants readily admitted to the deeds they were accused of, claiming in their defense that they were just following orders.

The Allied powers, displaying all the moral superiority that victory affords, held that simply following orders, which came to be known as the

Nuremberg defense, was no excuse for horrific behavior. Twelve of the defendants were sentenced to death. From these trials arose the Nuremberg principles, a set of guidelines created by the International Law Commission of the United Nations to codify the legal doctrines established in the trials. Principle IV states: "The fact that a person acted pursuant to order of his government or of a superior does not relieve him from responsibility under international law, provided a moral choice was in fact possible to him." In other words, being a bureaucrat, whether you're Adolf Eichmann or the clerk behind the counter at the motor vehicle administration, does not free you from the moral obligation or legal responsibility to do the right thing. Followers are accountable, too.

At the risk of defending Nazis, recent research has shown that there just might be something to the Nuremberg defense. A 2016 study published in the journal *Current Biology* found that people actually do feel disconnected from what they're doing when they are just following orders. The study found that under these conditions people experience their actions more as "passive movements than fully voluntary actions." Dr. Emilie Caspar, a cognitive neuroscientist and one of the study's co-authors said, "Our study shows that people under orders may not feel responsible for what they do. Perhaps that explains why so many people appeared to obey coercive orders… Our findings have several practical implications. First, maybe people can be trained to feel more responsible: that might allow them to resist orders that are inappropriate."

Blind obedience creates a sense of helplessness among its adherents. Demagogues, dictators, and loutish shift supervisors even actively encourage this feeling among their followers and subordinates. The political philosopher and author of *Eichmann in Jerusalem: A Report on the Banality of Evil,* Hannah Arendt, wrote of this, "Perhaps the nature of every bureaucracy is to make functionaries and mere cogs in the administrative machinery out of men, and thus to dehumanize them."

It's this fundamental, dehumanizing nature of organizations that effective followers are trying to counter. You can't expect leadership to change. It's been working pretty well for the folks at the top since before the time of the great pyramids. It's followership that has to adapt. Any new followership paradigm needs to be empowering, of course. But first and foremost, it must be humanizing.

Clearly the best way to effect positive change in any organization or society for that matter is to remind people that they are accountable human beings. They are responsible for their actions even when those actions are directed by others above them. With accountability comes awareness, which is always the first step in the process of change. So why hasn't there been more of an emphasis on responsible followership in the world of organizational development? After all, real transformation comes from the bottom up, not from the top down. It's because of leaders – abetted by the $14 billion a year leadership industry. They've made it all about themselves. I believe that followers are driven to follow as much as leaders are driven to lead. Yet all we hear about is leadership, leadership, leadership. Enough already!

In spite of what we've been led (by leaders) to believe, it's perfectly fine not to aspire to a leadership role. You're not alone if you don't want to be the leader- in fact you're in the majority. In 2014, CareerBuilder surveyed 3,625 workers nationwide representing a range of companies, industries, and salary levels and found that two-thirds of them did *not* desire a leadership position as a career goal. Most of these people (52 percent) said they were satisfied in their current positions; 34 percent didn't want their work/life balance to suffer; and 17 percent said they didn't have the education required for leadership. The survey also found that women are far more likely than men not to aspire to a leadership role (71 percent of women versus 60 percent of men).

It's not enough to say about leadership that, like macramé, Australian Rules football, and My Little Pony, it's a subject that you're just not interested in pursuing. It's helpful to understand why. When I started my career, I remember looking at my supervisor's job and thinking, "Wow. That's *not* what I want to be doing in five years." The things she dealt with (constituent complaints, deadlines, me, the big bosses, etc.) were not fun. They actually terrified me. I didn't acknowledge it at the time, to myself or anyone else, but I couldn't imagine myself in that role because I lacked confidence. What

25-year-old Geoff didn't understand was that most people feel the same way and that confidence is gained through experience.

Self-doubt is no excuse for not pursuing leadership. As a matter of fact, it's just the opposite. Self-doubt is a sign of humility and intelligence, both excellent qualities in a leader. If you're not pursuing leadership because you don't think you're ready, here's something to consider: YOU'LL NEVER THINK YOU'RE READY. That underlying fear of being outed as not smart enough or not experienced enough or not talented enough is so pervasive there's an official name for it: the imposter syndrome. A 2011 study published in the *International Journal of Behavioral Science* found that an estimated "70 percent of people will experience at least one episode of imposter syndrome in their lives." People with imposter syndrome feel like frauds. They carry with them an underlying belief that they're not as good as people think they are, and that they're undeserving of their workplace status. People with imposter syndrome take humility, a refreshing trait in any coworker, and turn it on its head.

There are many, many good reasons for not wanting to aspire to leadership. For me, I enjoy developing ideas and working on projects more than developing people and leading projects. I find fulfillment playing a supportive role to management in the organization. Leaders sometimes have trouble relating to the effective followership perspective, and, as a result, undervalued followers and their contributions to the team.

Well, enough is enough. The stigma stops now, and here it goes. "Hello. My name is Geoff and I am a follower, a born follower. I've always been a follower. As long as I can remember, I've been under the direction of somebody. I don't have to be the leader, but I will when it's necessary. I'm happiest when I'm a valued, respected member of a team, and I can see how my contributions further its mission, which I support whole heartedly."

Don't get me wrong. I won't just follow anybody or anything. I'm talking about effective followership - decidedly *not* the followership of bridge jumpers, Heaven's Gate cult members, or Nazi yes men like Adolf Eichmann. It's the followership of responsibility and self-actualization. It's the followership of the Buddha's four noble truths and eightfold path to enlightenment.

It's the followership of the Apostles of Christ (with the noted exception of Judas Iscariot). It's the followership of Arjuna in The Bhagavid Gita. It's the followership of kindness, compassion, and empathy. It's a followership for the twenty-first century and beyond.

Are you with me? Then stand up and say it aloud. "I, *state your name*, am a proud and responsible follower. It's my dedication to leadership's vision that makes it a reality. Without me and my ilk, there would be no Panama Canal, Great Pyramid of Giza, rock music festivals, or likes on Facebook. Twitter users would be sending their 280 characters out into a cyberspace void. Without followers, the world would be a very sad and desolate place. I mean, even more so."

There now. That wasn't so bad. Remember, every revolution starts small, sometimes with just a single follower. Or to re-phrase Karl Marx, "Followers of the world, unite. You have nothing to lose but your leaders."

CHAPTER 2:

Riding Down the Primrose Path in the Backseat of the People's Car

NAZI SS MOTTO: "My honor is called loyalty."

ME: "Devotion to an organization that doesn't appreciate or deserve you isn't loyalty; it's lunacy."

Diesel engines are dirty, stinky, sooty, and produce the pollutant nitrogen oxide (NO) in greater quantities than standard gasoline engines. Diesels do have some advantages over gas engines including greater durability and more miles per gallon, but their exhaust issues have always been a drawback to their more widespread popularity, especially in this age of climate-woke consumers. In the early 2000s Volkswagen, in its quest to become the biggest automobile company in the world, seized on the idea that featuring its fuel-efficient diesel engines would propel it past Toyota in its race to the top.

But first, VW engineers had to overcome that pesky problem with NO emissions. This was going to be a tough one. Catalytic converters, which work so well with gas engines to reduce NO, don't do nearly as well with diesel. VW considered buying the rights to the BlueTec technology, which was used by Mercedes for reducing pollution in its diesel vehicles, but decided against it because it was costly, required a lot of consumer maintenance, and was unproven in the long haul. VW engineers eventually developed their own method for making diesel engines run cleaner, which involved adding a liquid they called AdBlue to the exhaust. But this would have required VW owners to bring their cars in for maintenance much more often, which company management decided would be a deal breaker for consumers.

Volkswagen's new diesel motors in their present state were not going to pass strict American emissions testing standards. But yet – somehow- they did. And in late 2008, Volkswagen began a marketing campaign in the U.S., pushing the "clean diesel" technology of its Golf, Jetta, and Beetle models as an ecofriendly alternative to hybrids. Things were going swimmingly for Volkswagen until 2014.

It was then that a group of environmentalists from a small non-profit organization, the International Council on Clean Transportation (ICCT), released the findings of their report commissioned after they posed a simple and obvious question: Why do VW diesel cars in the U.S. run so much cleaner than those same cars in Europe? The ICCT found that these cars, when tested on the road, emitted up to 40 times the allowable level of harmful NO gas. Yet strangely in the laboratory, under controlled conditions, the cars passed all emissions tests. At first, the ICCT thought their instruments were faulty. But they eventually came to the conclusion that something was rotten in the state of Farfegnugen.

The EPA and the California Air Resources Board soon opened their own inquiries into the matter. After first stonewalling these groups, on September 3, 2015 Volkswagen admitted that their U.S. diesel cars came standard with an ingenious software package that allowed them to beat the tests. The cars could somehow sense when they were undergoing emissions testing through measurements of their speed, engine operations, and even the movement of the steering wheel, and switched to running in an underpowered mode that reduced exhaust emissions. When the cars were back on the road, the software switched them back to normal operations where they ran at full power and spewed pollutants like nobody's business.

OMG. Dozens of people, probably more, must have had direct knowledge of the software cheat and many more must have at least heard rumors of it, yet of the nearly 600,000 Volkswagen employees worldwide, not one came forward to blow the whistle on this stinkfest. I hate to pick on the Germans again, but this looks like the Nuremberg defense all over- except that Volkswagen management said that it wasn't *their* orders the employees were following. Michael Horn, the CEO of Volkswagen's American division testified before Congress in 2017 that "This was not a corporate decision. This was a couple of software engineers who put this in place for whatever reason." He added that VW had not been able to identify who these engineers might be or how many might have been involved, but they're going to get to the bottom of it.

No surprise here, but academic studies concluded that, in spite of what VW management said, although the scandal may have been carried out by rogue employees, it certainly wasn't caused by them. Jae C. Jung and Alison Park of the University of Missouri -Kansas City identified factors at VW that created a corporate climate conducive for such dishonest behavior, the most influential of which was the harsh leadership style of its management. For a company whose name literally translates as People's Car, Volkswagen didn't treat its people very well.

Jung and Park write that Ferdinand Piëch, grandson of the creator of the Beetle, Ferdinand Porsche, who served as the company's CEO for 10 years until 2002, "was notorious for his toxic leadership style in managing his employees by being authoritarian and coercive. His influence over his successors continued." Executives at the company were quickly dismissed or demoted for making mistakes or falling short. There was little to no autonomy granted to subordinates. Communication across and up and down the management hierarchy was discouraged. Failure was not an option at Volkswagen. Even though management's strategy of focusing on diesel instead of hybrid technology was doomed from the start, in that culture, the expectation was that employees would somehow make it work.

I find the Volkswagen scandal disturbing. It's hard for me to fathom that an organization as large and as well-respected and established as VW could be rife with that much duplicity. But apparently it's not uncommon for followers to be pressured by their leaders into committing illegal acts. If it happened at the number two car company in the world, it certainly could happen at your workplace.

As effective followers, we try to find win-win resolutions to workplace conflicts, but in these situations there are only losers. If you were tasked with writing code to circumvent emissions testing and were never caught and even received a pay raise for your work, could you still feel good about yourself? Maybe. But what happens when the deception is uncovered? Followers beware. Leaders will lead you astray, then throw you under the Microbus to save themselves when the jig is up. It's just what they do.

The first person sentenced in the VW scandal wasn't the CEO or an executive vice president. It was a software engineer, James Liang, who was fined $200,000 and given over three years of jail time. "He wasn't the mastermind," his attorney said. Liang was a loyal company man who chose not to walk away from his job or expose the deception. An unsympathetic Federal judge found him to be "too loyal" to Volkswagen and handed down a lengthier sentence than prosecutors recommended.

Oliver Schmidt, who headed the company's U.S. environmental and engineering office, wrote in a letter to the judge at his sentencing, "I must say that I feel misused by my own company." He said that he had come on board only after the scheme had been implemented. Invoking the Nuremberg defense once again, he claimed that he was misled by his supervisors and was just following a script written by management when he lied to regulators.

The Volkswagen scandal should serve as a cautionary tale for followers everywhere. Martin Winterkorn, CEO of the automaker at the time of the emissions cheating, has not been convicted of anything. He walks the earth a free man and so far is keeping the tens of millions of dollars he earned in bonuses. Oliver Schmidt meanwhile sits in a Federal prison serving a seven-year sentence.

At the risk of virtue signaling, I think the answer is simple if the boss asks you to do something illegal or unethical: NO. But perhaps I'm being a bit unrealistic, and the answer is actually more complicated than that. Sooner or later, all followers are placed in that difficult situation where they're asked to bend the rules. It may be something small like extending the deadline on a job posting so the boss's niece can apply. It might be something huge like changing students' answers on a standardized test. Or it might be something in-between like installing software on two machines when the license agreement allows for only one.

It's up to you what you do in these situations. I'm not judging. But regardless of your decision, self-protection should be your overriding concern. Simply flat-out refusing a direct order is insubordination, which can be grounds for termination - not that your employer actually needs a cause to get rid of you. Workers in the U.S. are considered by default to be "at-will" employees, which means they can be fired at any time for almost any reason or for no reason whatsoever. Seriously.

There are a few narrow exceptions to the doctrine of at will employment. Title VII of the Civil Rights Act of 1964 and related laws prohibit termination for reasons related to age, race, color, national origin, religion, gender, disability, pregnancy, genetic information, etc. An employer also may not fire an employee if it conflicts with a well-established public policy. For example, in most states, an employee can't be terminated just because he or she files a workers' comp claim or an EEOC complaint. Workers represented by unions, too, are often covered by employment contracts that trump at will employment.

Common law protects employees from termination for refusing to perform an illegal act. But good luck suing your employer for wrongful discharge. The burden of proof falls squarely on the employee in these cases, and it's a pretty big burden. First off, the act must be illegal under criminal law, and you didn't do it. And your refusal to perform the act must be the *sole and only* reason for your firing. So if your last performance evaluation was so-so plus you refused to put cyanide in an auditor's coffee mug, you have no recourse when you're let go. Same holds if you've been tardy a few times and politely declined when told to double charge Medicare for a procedure that wasn't performed.

Quick tips for when the boss asks you to do something illegal or unethical:

1. Jiminy Cricket. Give it some thought before you agree to do something for the boss that your mom and dad wouldn't approve of. Channel that Zen master spiritual guru Jiminy Cricket who instructed his devotees, when faced with a life altering decision, to "give a little whistle. And always let your conscience be your guide."

2. Know which way the wind blows. Be sure that what you're being tasked with is actually illegal or unethical and not just something you don't want to do. You may have very good reasons for disagreeing with the boss. (It's bad for business. It's unreasonable. It's weird. She's weird.) But don't make this about you. Ask a trusted colleague, do a little online research, or refer to the organization's policies if you need to confirm that the activity is illegal or unethical.

3. I'd love to, but... Don't offer excuses for why you can't comply with the request. (My dog ate my laptop. I'm too busy with the Stevens case. I'm having Botox that day.) Bosses will find a way to work around your pretext, then you'll be stuck in the awkward position of having to admit that it was just an excuse and that your real answer is, "Hell no!"

4. Play stupid. Pretend like you don't quite understand what the boss is saying, and ask her to repeat the request, or better yet, ask her to send it to you in an email. Ask pointed questions of your supervisor like, "Let me get this straight. You want me to change the third quarter income statement to show we've met our earnings goal? Why would I do that?" Most managers will back down at that point.

5. Document. Document. Document. If your boss is insistent, then record your response in writing. Be brief but factual, explaining that you won't be complying with his request because it is illegal and/or unethical. Record the dates and times of your conversations with the boss and exactly what was said by whom. Your boss is going to claim later that you misunderstood him. It is helpful in these instances to have a verbatim transcript recorded shortly after the conservation occurred. Keep it in a safe place, with a backup copy offsite.

6. Stand your ground. Your boss should be nervous. He knows that you know what you were told to do was wrong, and no amount of bullying and intimidation is going to make you back down. From this point onward, he won't trust you and it probably won't be a fun place to work anymore, but if you want to stay, by all means, stay. You did nothing wrong. But keep your résumé up-to-date and an empty box under your desk just in case.

A far more common and difficult situation followers find themselves in is when the boss asks them to do something unreasonable or that doesn't make sense. If it's the latter, you owe it to your boss and to your organization (and to yourself) to understand the why, what, and how of that new assignment. Don't assume the boss is going to tell you these things from the get-go or that his vagueness is intentional. Management tends to undervalue communication and how important it is that employees understand their mission. When you don't know or understand the particulars of an assignment or the assignment itself appears to be illogical or counterproductive, a conversation with the boss is warranted.

The key is creating the right context for this conversation. The context you are trying for is one of a sincere employee with the best interests of the organization at heart using the Socratic Method to ensure that management has considered certain potential liabilities in its decision making. The one you want to avoid is a PITA (pain-in-the-ass) employee whining about another change in the way things used to be done around here.

You are asking questions about the assignment, soliciting advice from your boss- not questioning his authority, knowledge, or judgement. And remember, there's no such thing as a stupid question. Carl Sagan, the great science communicator, said, "Every question is a cry to understand the world." Select a time and place for the conversation so that it presents as little a threat as possible to your manager. Use a deferential tone. Listen nonjudgmentally. Smile. Even with all this, bosses are going to get defensive when they're asked questions, especially insightful ones that raise points they hadn't considered before. But don't let this dissuade you. The upside of asking (becoming a trusted, valued colleague, protecting the organization, etc.) far outweighs the down. Besides, what would we be if we didn't try?

And there's an added benefit to seeking advice from your boss; it makes you look smarter. A 2014 study conducted by researchers at the Harvard Business School suggests that soliciting advice doesn't cast you as ignorant or stupid - just the opposite. The researchers concluded that "not only is advice-seeking beneficial for the spread of information, but it may also boost perceptions of competence for advice seekers and make advisors feel affirmed."

In addition to feeling flattered that you sought him out, your boss will recognize that you're smart enough to know that you don't know everything and even smarter still for figuring out the right person to go to. Him! Seeking advice reveals some vulnerability, too, which should build trust and strengthen the work relationship between you and the boss.

Warning: Don't go around the office asking everyone for their advice unless you plan to actually take it. This approach will backfire according to Hayley Blunden of the Harvard Business School and co-author of the study, *The Interpersonal Costs of Ignoring Advice*. He said, "Research shows that those whose advice you don't take may have a worse view of you afterward. They may even see you as less competent or avoid you." For those you do ask, thank them for their input and follow up with them later to let them know how things turned out. That's my advice.

Effective followers make their bosses better leaders. Often the reason you're not clear about the assignment is because *they're* not clear about it. Asking them the right questions encourages bosses to focus, analyze, and more fully form their plan so that they can better articulate it. This requires followers to have the ability to think beyond their own cubicles. This is a rare skill indeed. Adopting a sympathetic mindset toward management and combining it with their own unique frontline perspective allows effective followers to identify potential pitfalls their leaders may never have considered.

Quick tips about what to ask the boss when you're assigned a new project:

1. You want it when? You need to know the due date and the consequences if it's not finished by the deadline. Does she want it on her desk by the end of the day or by the end times? What's her expectation for the project timeline? Will late papers be accepted? Will they be dropped by one letter grade for each day they're late?

2. What's the purpose of this thing? And just as important, who's my audience? You need to know the endgame. A plan, no matter how beautifully researched and executed, is useless if it doesn't work towards the goal. It then becomes a solution in search of a problem.

Say for instance you've been assigned to develop a program for sexual harassment prevention at your workplace. It's essential that you understand why management is so interested in developing such a program now. If it's because a supervisor pooh-poohed the repeated complaints of graduate student interns about the lascivious comments of a certain boss's nephew, a portion of your program must address the responsibilities of supervisors when such things are brought to their attention. (And what constitutes a hostile work environment.)

3. What do you want from me? It's all about expectations, tempering them if you can. When the work is completed you want to be sure that there are no surprises or misunderstandings in terms of what's been expected of you. If you're not sure, now is the time to ask. If you don't know the expectations, how can you exceed them?

4. Who else will I be working with? You need to know who the stakeholders are on the project and who you can go to if you need assistance. As an effective follower, you appreciate how crucial it is to establish lines of communication among team members. Projects can be a great conduit for establishing effective work relationships. A supervisor once told me years ago after my promotion, "This work is all about relationships. Build them in the good times, because you're going to need them in the bad."

As an effective follower, you are going to be overwhelmed with work assignments from time to time. Managers tend to overburden their best employees and work around the PITAs. I call this "the curse of competence." Saying no to the boss is fraught with peril and should not be undertaken lightly, but it's worth a try when you feel you're approaching your breaking point. Reasonable bosses can make unreasonable requests. And after all, politely declining a new assignment is still better for you in the long run than taking it on and failing miserably. I once told my supervisor after she assigned me additional responsibilities, "But my plate is full." To which she replied, "Here, let me get you a bigger plate."

Quick tips for saying no to the boss:

1. The sooner the better. Please don't wait until the project's due date to tell your boss that it's just not your thing. Schedule a meeting with her at the earliest opportunity. Every minute that passes between when you're assigned the job and when you decline it makes it that much harder to extricate yourself from the situation.

2. You got this. Don't say no because you believe you're not up to the challenge. Your modesty is an endearing quality, but don't let it hold you back. Your boss has confidence in you (if she didn't, she wouldn't have assigned you the job), I have confidence in you, you need to have confidence in you. Don't let the amount of work scare you off either. Hard work never killed anybody. Or maybe it did. It doesn't really matter.

3. Be prepared. Have some notes prepared when you present your case on why you're not the man (or woman) for the job. But focus on work reasons, not the personal ones. Don't mention your best friend's destination wedding coming up unless you've already asked off for those dates. It's what's best for the organization that matters.

4. Put it in the pile with the others. Say yes to the job, but then ask your boss to help you prioritize the projects you're currently working on. Where does this new one fit in? Which ones should be relegated to back burner if you have to take on one more thing? She'll get the point.

5. Think like a leader. Offer the boss alternatives. Maybe the job can be postponed until after the busy season. Maybe it would be a great learning opportunity for the new guy. Heck, you'll even work with the new guy on this. Presenting possibilities shows that you've given this some thought, and it's not just about you saying no.

CHAPTER 3:

Rule One: The Boss is Never Wrong.
Rule Two: When the Boss is Wrong,
See Rule One.

DOUGLAS MacARTHUR:
"You are remembered for the rules you break."

ME: "Just because you've never been good at following rules
doesn't make you a natural born leader."

On March 2, 2020, the country was fast approaching DEFCON 1 on its media fueled frenzied ride to a full blown panic mode reaction to the impending coronavirus epidemic. President Donald Trump, attempting to calm the nation's jitters, held a press briefing where he trotted out scientists and pharmaceutical company executives to echo his administration's message not to worry because they've got this. When asked about a timeline for a vaccine, Trump responded, "I've heard very quick numbers, that of months. And I've heard pretty much a year would be an outside number. So I think that's not a bad range. But if you're talking about three to four months in a couple of cases, a year in other cases."

This was just what the nation wanted to hear. So what if it wasn't true? Everyone on the dais that day knew the timeline wasn't accurate. It was widely acknowledged among the experts that it would take at least eighteen months before a vaccine for this new strain of the coronavirus could be made widely available. The "three to four months" range Trump was referencing was the timeframe to develop a test vaccine. Trump was clearly mistaken here. But would any of the scientists or executives speak up? Why would they? Why should they?

When you weigh the full blunt trauma of Trump's wrath (he hated to be contradicted) against the need for the American people to have accurate information about a looming health crisis, the president's wrath will win out every time. Every time, but this one. Dr. Anthony Fauci, the head of the National Institute of Allergy and Infectious Diseases, immediately chimed in with his more realistic estimate for the vaccine timeline. Trump folded his arms across his chest and looked on disapprovingly as the doctor spoke.

When Fauci finished, Trump asked the group, "Do you think that's right?" Yes, they responded, reluctantly. Leonard Schleifer, the CEO of Regeneron Pharmaceuticals, said the process is time-consuming because "vaccines have to be tested because there's precedent for vaccines to actually make diseases worse. ... You don't want to rush and treat a million people and find out you're making 900,000 of them worse." That would be a bad thing.

I'm not saying that Fauci is a hero or courageous or even an effective follower for contradicting his boss, the leader of the free world, in public. In this case, the good doctor falls somewhere between being outright insubordinate and someone who's been around so long they don't care anymore about their career or what the boss thinks. Fauci was 79 years old at the time and had been on the job through six presidents, all kinds of outbreaks, and 35 years.

Fauci anticipated this scenario and his response to the president was entirely premeditated. Three days prior to the press briefing, he said in an interview, "You should never destroy your own credibility. And you don't want to go to war with a president. But you've got to walk the fine balance of making sure you continue to tell the truth." Correcting your boss in public is a lot easier when you're 79 years old with 35 years of distinguished service under your belt. But what about for the rest of us? What do you do when your boss makes a big slip-up at an important client meeting? And you need your job. Do you speak up? Well, do you?

It's a risky proposition, one that's going to call on the full force of your heightened emotional intelligence quotient to resolve. There's a lot to consider and a lot at stake. You have to think critically, and you have to think fast, which can be mutually exclusive tasks in times of stress. But maybe it's not as complicated as all that. Maybe the decision of what to do in these situations rests entirely on the answer to one simple question: Is this the hill I want to die on?

If the boss's mistake involves misquoting a Jimi Hendrix song ("Scuse me while I kiss this guy") or a line from his favorite Bill Murray movie ("Did you get a free bowl of soup with that hat? But on you it looks good"), maybe that's not your hill. If you're an operating room nurse and your boss is a surgeon, your response might be a little different. Or maybe not.

A 2016 Johns Hopkins study concluded that medical errors were the third leading cause of death in the United States, trailing only heart disease and cancer. Hospitals can be downright dangerous. A quarter of a million Americans die each year due to preventable medical mistakes. The researchers found that most of these deaths aren't because of inherently bad doctors, nurses, and medical techs. Rather, they say, most mistakes are the result of systemic failures. One of the biggest of these is a culture that elevates the status of doctors at the expense of all others. This has a chilling effect on the willingness of subordinates to speak up when they witness protocols being ignored or errors being made, even when the consequences of their silence are dire.

A study by the American Association of Critical Care Nurses (AACCN) and others, titled "The Silent Treatment," found that more than 80% of nurses have felt denigrated when they tried to point out to a physician or other clinician that there was a potential issue with their treatment or prescription. The deck is stacked against nurses in these situations. The system has historically protected physicians' jobs while making nurses vulnerable. The result is that physicians are much less likely to have their decisions or actions questioned or to take to heart any of the constructive criticism they may receive.

Alexandra Robbins, the author of *The Nurses: A Year of Secrets, Drama, and Miracles with the Heroes of the Hospital,* said that one of the most surprising discoveries she made while researching her book was the great number of nurses who have witnessed or been the victims of bullying by doctors. In fact, she found in her interviews with hundreds of nurses from across the country that one of the hardest parts of the profession was having to deal with Dr. Pompous, M.D. According to the Joint Commission, an independent organization that evaluates and accredits health care organizations, this bullying creates a hostile work environment, but maybe more importantly, it's a contributing factor in medical errors, increased health care costs, and decreased quality of patient care.

It seems that not much has changed since 1967, when psychiatrist Leonard Stein coined the term "the doctor–nurse game" to refer to this imbalance of power in their workplace relationship. He found that nurses had to tread carefully so as to not upset the hierarchy. They had to make suggestions subtly and gently and even in a manner to suggest that their recommendations were actually the doctor's idea. Everything they did was part of an elaborate kabuki dance of deference to the overwhelmingly male doctors' sense of professional dominance. Stein said that for the nurses who refused to play the game, there was "hell to pay" and that they might be "unconsciously suffering from penis envy."

This dynamic between surgeons and nurses in the operating room is evocative of the one years ago between pilots and copilots in Korean Airlines cockpits as described by Malcolm Gladwell in his book *Outliers*. "Korean Air had more plane crashes than almost any other airline in the world for a period at the end of the 1990s," Gladwell said. This wasn't because their planes were old or badly maintained or because their pilots were inexperienced or unskilled. No, argued Gladwell, it was because of the rigid, hierarchical structure of Korean society, which demands deferential treatment of elders and superiors in a way that's far beyond the expectations in the West.

This cultural legacy directly clashed with the design of modern, complex aircraft which required a captain and his copilot to operate the craft as equals. The results for Korean Airlines were catastrophic. Gladwell said that plane crashes tend to occur because of an accumulation of little issues, any of which on their own would not be enough to bring down a plane. "The typical accident involves seven consecutive human errors," he said. Even given seven opportunities, copilots would often fail to alert their superiors of their concerns.

Unlike the medical community, the aviation industry, and Korean Airlines in particular, addressed this issue, but only after acknowledging the inherent problems of a culture where the leader is above reproach. Copilots are now expected to bring potential issues to their captain's attention and escalate their concerns if the captain fails to respond in a satisfactory manner. Captains, equally, are expected to listen openly, acknowledge, and address the concerns of their subordinates. Korean Airlines is now one of the safest carriers in the world.

Wouldn't it be nice if all workplace environments were as receptive to leader-follower collaboration as a Korean Airlines Boeing 767 cockpit? But back here in coach, telling your manager he's wrong is still a dicey proposition.

Quick tips for setting the boss straight:

1. Be right. First and foremost, before you get yourself all in a lather about how to correct the boss, be damn sure he's wrong and you're right. Managers often possess information that their subordinates aren't privy to. Make absolutely sure that you heard him correctly and that he is mistaken. Undertake a little fact-checking mission if you have to in order to confirm your suspicion. You don't want the tables to be turned and that you're the one who ends up getting set straight.

2. Is this the hill you want to die on? What's really at stake here? Is it just your ego's need for validation or has the boss mistakenly promised the country a vaccine in four months' time that could take at least a year to roll out to the general public? If the leader's error is a costly one, by all means, proceed with caution. If it's not, treat him with the same amount of respect you'd appreciate receiving after committing a mistake.

3. Avoid correcting him in public. Telling your boss he was wrong in front of his boss, his boss's boss, or a client is a career kamikaze move. Even if your heart is pure and your intentions are golden, even if you work for the Dalai Lama, even if he told you to correct him anytime he's wrong, this act should be undertaken only when absolutely necessary. If you're in a big meeting (and you can tell it's a big one because he's wearing a necktie and/or socks) and the boss makes a fatal error, first try using body language or subtle facial clues to convey something is amiss. Or print your concern in five words or less on a notepad and hold it in your boss's sightline. If it's a virtual meeting, send the boss a quick message.

If that doesn't get the job done, then speak up. Start by asking for permission to address the group about the issue. Speak respectfully and in a nonthreatening tone. You may even present your concern as a question. Be prepared to be dismissed quickly or get cutoff in midsentence. Stay professional and don't take it too personally. Got it?

4. It's not what you say; it's how you say it. Of all my wonderful qualities, I think it's my humility that sets me above others the most. That and my tremendous sense of irony. It's hard not to appear a little smug in these delicate conversations with leadership when you know you're right and they've screwed up. But try to rein in the self-satisfaction. A humble mindset will help to ensure that your words are spoken with a kind intonation and received and accepted in that spirit. There's a right and a wrong way to say, "I told you so" and saying, "I told you so" is decidedly the wrong way. Presenting your correction as a suggestion or as an opinion is also a good way of making sure it falls on receptive ears.

5. Offer a solution. Don't just point out the error in his ways. Anybody can do that. Heck, criticizing the stupidity of those around you is the fun part of any job. Developing and implementing a practical, reasonable solution – now that's work. But that's what effective followers do. They often know the intricacies of the business operations better than their managers, which makes them uniquely qualified to develop workable solutions. By offering a resolution, you can shift the focus of the conversation from how the boss screwed up to how things can be made right. That alone should put you on the short list for the Nobel Prize in Followership.

6. How about never? Is never good for you? Bad news rarely gets better with age. Still it's important to choose the right moment for that heart-to-heart. A Friday afternoon, payday, with a holiday Monday can be good. The first thing on that Tuesday morning back? Not so much. Ideally, it should be a private setting, one where you can have each other's undivided attention. Just don't let too much time pass between the boss's faux pas and your meeting with him about it. The half-life of these things is short. The 24-hour news cycle is down to 12 hours. For office gaffes, it can be an even shorter timeframe before everybody's on to the next calamity.

7. Taking it to the next level. Don't think you're going to be hailed as a hero if you blow the whistle on a supervisor error, even one that jeopardizes the health and safety of Labradoodle puppies. (They're so adorable.) Nobody likes bad news or its bearers. If your conversation with the boss didn't meet your expectations, you have a decision to make.

But before you take this to the next level, be absolutely sure this is an actual error you're exposing. Don't make this about you! If it turns out to be just you thinking you know better than your boss how the organization should be run, it's not going to end well. The human resources office may be a good place to start before going to your boss's boss. Before meeting with them, confidentially if you can, document your concerns in writing, sticking to the facts. Include information about your meetings with your supervisor and what was said by whom. I can't stress this enough: Do not make this about you. Focus on the organization and how best to protect it.

8. Let it go, Elsa. Sometimes you have to accept the fact that leadership is going to do what it wants regardless. I'm proud of you for gathering the courage to make your boss aware of a potential problem caused by something he's said or done. Organizations, even society as a whole, would be a lot better off if more followers had the wherewithal to take this leap. As we've seen, unquestioned authority plus time equals catastrophe.

Your conscience should be clear now and you should have no regrets. But if the whole thing still makes you feel uneasy, (and singing karaoke from the *Frozen* soundtrack is not an option) try reciting the serenity prayer: God, grant me the serenity to accept the things I cannot change, / The courage to change the things I can, / And the wisdom to know the difference, / And God, grant this to me now because I'm in kind of a hurry. (That last line was added by me.)

Along with a copy of the serenity prayer, keep all your documentation about the incident in a secure place. Leaders tend to have short and selective memories about these sorts of things.

CHAPTER 4:

How to Start a Dance Craze
Over Brunch

JILL JACKSON: "Let there be peace on earth
and let it begin with me."

ME: "Why me? Why does it always have to be me?"

One of the all-time most popular TED talks also happens to be one
of the shortest and simplest of the genre. Clocking in at just about three
minutes, *How to Start a Movement*, first presented in 2010, is essentially just
grainy, shaky video of spectators at a music festival, with voiceover commentary by Derek Sivers, a music entrepreneur. (Check it out.) The video begins
with a barefoot, shirtless guy dancing awkwardly on a grassy hill. (Think
Elaine Benes on Red Bull.) He doesn't seem to care that he's the only one
dancing; he's just really into the music. Sivers provides the play-by-play as
the shirtless guy is joined in the dancing by his first follower, then by another,
and another, and another. Within a couple of minutes, people are rushing in
from all over to get in on the fun. The group starts to grow to the point where
it's the people on the sidelines, who haven't joined in the dancefest, who've
become the odd men out.

Sivers used the video to illustrate his concept of the First Follower. He posits that the basis for starting any kind of initiative that's even a little outside of the mainstream is to attract that first diehard, passionate adherent. According to Sivers, a movement's first follower is as vital to its propagation as its initiator. "The first follower is what transforms a lone nut into a leader," he said. It's that first follower, sticking his neck out for everyone to see, who makes it possible for all the others to join in. "New followers emulate other followers- not the leader," Silvers said. He believes that leaders should accept their first follower as an equal because each is equally as essential in achieving their common purpose.

I know what you're thinking. The First Follower Concept no doubt applies to a bunch of dancing, molly-popping hipsters at Burning Man, but what about for the rest of us back on Planet Earth? What does it have to do with me enjoying Sunday brunch with some friends at our neighborhood greasy spoon? Funny you should ask.

Researchers from the University of Washington studied what people ate for brunch and came up with an interesting conclusion, one that supports Sivers and his First Follower Concept. From June to August of 2016, data regarding the menu items ordered for brunch on Saturdays and Sundays at a local restaurant were collected and analyzed. The data included the food items ordered at each table by each diner, the seat number of each diner, and the order in which each diner at the table placed his order with the wait staff.

The researchers' findings, published in the paper *Is the Follower the Leader? How the First Follower Establishes the Group Norm in Sequential Behavior*, demonstrated that what the second person at the table, i.e. the first follower, ordered influenced all the food items subsequently ordered at the table. When the first follower ordered an entree similar to what the first person ordered (a Caesar salad after a chef's salad, say) the other diners at the table tended to also order similar menu items. If the first follower ordered a bacon double cheeseburger and a beer, however, after the first person ordered a house salad and water, the other orders at the table tended to continue this trend of variety. The first follower signals to the rest of the group whether it's OK or not to be different.

The research paper states, "These results indicate that when the first follower orders similarly to the leader, the group norm becomes uniformity. When the group norm is to seek uniformity, the rest of the group is more likely to order similarly. However, when the first follower orders differently from the leader, this causes the group norm to be variety-seeking. When the group norm is to seek variety, there will be more diversity in the table's ordering patterns. Taken together, these results indicate that the first follower's actions relative to the leader determine whether the group norm will be to seek variety or uniformity." (I don't know about you, but I'm much more inclined to order a Bloody at brunch if I know that at least one other person at the table will be imbibing with me.)

The First Follower Concept may have also played a part in why people chose to eat at that restaurant in the first place. It turns out that crowd-sourced reviews share a lot in common with brunch orders. In 2017, researchers examined 179,774 Yelp reviews covering 8,091 businesses within the state of Pennsylvania. They found that when the review posted by the first follower aligns with that of the leader (first reviewer), "the perception of a common group opinion increases, and the review difference from the leader decreases." When the first follower's Yelp review differs from that of the leader, it's more likely that other reviewers will also present differing views and the perception that there's a consensus opinion of the business decreases.

In his TED talk, Sivers said, "The first follower is actually an underestimated form of leadership in itself." But as important as first followers are, you don't necessarily have to be one to become a positive influence on your organization. Any follower, the second, fifth, one-hundred and fifth or one thousandth can be a catalyst for change. It just takes the right intention. Or as my friend Glinda once told me after I had trouble returning from a particularly weird business trip to Oz, "You've always had the power my dear, you just had to learn it for yourself."

We can't count on leaders to create a hospitable workplace atmosphere. Grumps abound in their ranks. So followers have to take matters into their own hands. A single follower, just by being upbeat and joyful, can change the workplace culture of an entire organization. That's right. If you want your colleagues to feel better at work, despite the boss, all you have to do is radiate positivity and enthusiasm in their midst.

Research and history have confirmed time and again that emotions (the good, the bad, and the ugly) go viral quite easily. In a 1993 paper, psychologists Elaine Hatfield, John Cacioppo, and Richard Rapson coined the term "emotional contagion" to describe how the emotions and behaviors of one person can elicit the same emotions and behaviors in others. They define it as "the tendency to automatically mimic and synchronize expressions, vocalizations, postures, and movements with those of another person's and, consequently, to converge emotionally."

People naturally and subconsciously imitate the attitudes, expressions, and gestures of those around them. It's not just yawning that's contagious. Humans have a penchant for mirroring nearly every mannerism and mood put before them. ("Monkey see, monkey do," as the kids used to say.) The amazing part of this phenomenon is that our own internal emotional experiences are actually influenced by the nonverbal signals we imitate. When you smile, even if it's only in response to that guy in the next cubicle who's always smiling, you feel happier. When you glower back at an annoying coworker, you'll feel that on the inside, too.

The emotional contagion phenomenon can transform a workplace, and on rare occasions, it reveals just how powerful a force it can be. The June Bug Epidemic is a good example. In June of 1962, a few employees in the dressmaking unit of a textile mill in North Carolina started to get sick. Their flu-like symptoms included dizziness, numbness, and vomiting. Word quickly spread throughout the factory that the stricken employees had been bitten by some kind of bug or insect while at work, and that this was the cause of their illness. Cases continued to multiply until eventually 62 of the 900 workers at the plant came to assert they had been bitten by a bug and were experiencing similar symptoms. Many sought medical treatment; some required hospitalization.

The mill temporarily shut down as health officials and the Communicable Disease Center in Atlanta searched for the mysterious illness-causing creatures at the root of this mini-epidemic. But they came up empty. No evidence of the bugs was ever found, and work returned to normal at the plant. Investigators and officials eventually concluded that the most likely cause of the symptoms was anxiety, which spread from employee to employee like a novel coronavirus. No amount of handwashing or disinfecting wipes could have helped the situation. It was a work environment conducive to propagating uneasiness among its inhabitants as the mill had opened recently and had high production goals although managers and employees were still getting up to speed with things.

No doubt anxiety is contagious, but so is enthusiasm. It's up to you which one shapes your work environment. But what do you do if you don't feel that enthusiasm, that vim and vigor anymore? You can always fake it until you make it. I know it sounds bogus, but it's actually a proven strategy in psychotherapy. If you change your behavior, your thoughts and feelings will follow. To become a positive influence in your workplace, first start by acting more positive. You'll eventually find yourself not having to act anymore.

The key to "fake it until you make it" is that you have to be sincere about it. Seriously, your motivations must be genuine or you are going to come across as a big phony. You have to be invested in changing yourself, your thoughts, your feelings, your actions, your intentions, and not just in changing what others think about you.

There aren't any shortcuts. You can't start wearing nice new clothes and expensive jewelry to work, but keep the same behaviors and attitudes and expect things to improve. Research shows that this tack backfires. A 2015 study published in the *Journal of Consumer Research, Inc.* found that, "Consumers who use products to boost their sense of self-worth tend to dwell on their shortcomings and their ability to exert self-control is impaired." "Dress for the job you want, not the job you have" probably wasn't even helpful advice back in the *Mad Men* days when people wore trilby hats and galoshes to the office when it rained.

If a colleague said to you, "I've been noticing the way you work around here. And you know something? You're an effective follower." Would you take it as a complement? Should you? What if your boss told you the same thing? Would you modestly thank him? Or doth protest too much, methinks?

Effective follower. It's a cringe-worthy, left-handed appellation for sure. But at least it shows some appreciation for the skillset you're aspiring to. And if it's true, wear it proudly. Being an effective follower doesn't mean you're a manipulative phony. Or a subservient sycophant. Or an obsequious toady. (Thank you thesaurus.com.) It doesn't involve giving your supervisor a "World's Greatest Boss" coffee mug for his birthday or a bread maker for Christmas. Effective followers are not sheep; they are sharks in sheep's clothing (if you can picture that look.)

Ensuring that your boss is successful is good for you, your karma, your coworkers, your organization, and, of course, lastly your boss. It doesn't make you a suck up. It makes you a valued, respected member of the team. It makes you a professional. After all, it's what you're paid to do. If you dislike your boss so much that it pains you to see her succeed, get out. If you stay, support her. Respect her. I'm not saying you have to love, honor, and cherish her- just don't go out of your way to make her look bad.

There is absolutely nothing to be gained by making a bad boss look worse. If she's really that awful, she's probably doing a fine job all on her own of exposing her incompetence. It's your reputation that will suffer if you're found to be surreptitiously undermining her. And who needs the drama?

Making your boss successful lays the groundwork for your own success. It may not be immediate or even visible, but working to bring out the best in others is a reward unto itself. There's a special place in heaven for effective followers. It's between the volleyball courts and the waterpark, with easy access to the endless buffet. Or so I've heard.

If I had to reduce the essence of effective followership to two words, they would be "Command respect." If I were allowed seven, they would be "Command respect and don't be a jerk." But since I have a whole book to fill up, here goes: "Effective followership is the art of developing and maintaining productive working relationships with supervisors and colleagues in order to promote a positive influence on your organization and its members, clients, and products."

Please take out your fluorescent highlighter now and mark the words "working relationship" in the previous sentence. (It's probably going to be on the test.) Effective followership is not about becoming besties with the boss. In fact, I highly recommend against it. It's much easier to navigate the workplace when you set and keep boundaries between your personal and work lives. When your personal identity is too wrapped up in your job identity, not matter how great the job, you're setting yourself up for a fall. Besides, it's always a best practice to keep your work-spouse and your spouse-spouse apart from each other.

I know this flies in the face of every workplace TV sitcom ever, but your coworkers are *not* your family – in spite of what Mary Richards believes. In the final episode of the Mary Tyler Moore Show, Moore's character, Mary Richards, gave an iconic speech to her coworkers as they were about to leave the newsroom for the last time. "Well I just wanted you to know, that sometimes I get concerned about being a career woman," she began. "I get to thinking my job is too important to me. And I tell myself that the people I work with are just the people I work with, and not my family. And last night I thought, 'What is a family anyway?' They're just people who make you feel less alone and really loved. And that's what you've done for me. Thank you for being my family."

It was a poignant scene and a fitting ending to a beloved series, but that doesn't make it right. Separating work-family from family-family is as important as ever, but it's getting to be nearly impossible in today's environment. The line has become hopelessly blurred because of work-from-home and the constant barrage of emails and texts about work. In the course of a year, you probably spend as much time with your work-family as your family-family, but it's your family-family who suffers. Ask them how it makes them feel when you miss dinner because you're working late out of a sense of organizational-induced guilt or continually reply to work emails while spending "quality time" with them on a weekend. Ask anyone who's worked in a family-owned business about the pitfalls of mixing family and business. You can't go to work to escape family problems and you can't spend time with family to get away from work.

When your boss refers to his staff as "our work family," even if he's genuine, it can be a loaded, manipulative proposition. Alison Green, author of *Ask a Manager*, said in a 2018 interview, "'We're like a family here' tends to be used in ways that really disadvantage workers. It often means that boundaries get violated and people are expected to show inappropriate amounts of commitment and loyalty, even when it's not in their self-interest." A better analogy might be that your boss and coworkers are more like neighbors than family. You're happy to share a chat over the backyard fence or lend them your hedge clippers, but an extended stay on your living room couch is out of the question.

You don't have to work for a horrible boss or a terrible organization to reap the benefits of practicing effective followership. It can make any work situation better. The goal of effective followership is to nurture healthy work relationships so that you can be a positive force for good in your organization. And one of the best ways to do this is to do your job and to do it well.

Quick tips for practicing effective followership:

1. Cut him some slack. Bosses put themselves out there every day, making the tough decisions, often based on incomplete or faulty information, which sometimes don't turn out so well. They're doing the best that they can. Resist the schadenfreude and urge to publicly criticize or play Monday morning quarterback when things go south. Beneath the bravado and arrogance, deep down, bosses are just like you and me.

Bosses are like your kids in that they're who they are, not necessarily who you want them to be. Accept them, within reason, warts and all. And stop wishing they were somebody else instead. There's no such thing as the perfect boss; they're all just fallible human beings. A good way to remind yourself that she's human is to get to know a little about your boss as a person. You may have more in common than you thought, and it's hard to demonize someone who shares some of your same personality traits. Or at least it ought to be.

The worst thing you can do is carry around resentment and anger towards your boss or spouse or anyone for that matter. It's been said that harboring resentment is like ingesting poison and expecting the other person to get sick. If you can't let go of the bitterness, it's time to leave. Don't think that you can keep it bottled up and no one will notice. That animosity taints all of your interactions with the boss and finds its way to the surface at the most inopportune times. Let it go or leave.

That said, nobody deserves to work for a boss who is mean spirited, abusive, tyrannical, unethical, dishonest, or cruel. Nor should people remain in a work situation that compromises their physical or emotional well-being. Life is too short and your health is too precious to put up with that nonsense.

Since we're on the subject of boss appreciation, I can't resist the opportunity to vent a little about the absolute worst of the Hallmark holidays: Boss's Day. I feel the same way about Boss's Day as my parents felt about Children's Day. Every kid at one time or another asks his parents why there's a Mother's Day and a Father's Day, but not a Children's Day. And they answered, "Because every day is Children's Day." Same holds for Boss's Day.

The faux holiday was originated in 1958 by a woman who worked as a secretary for her father in his insurance agency. She thought that her dad's hard work and dedication wasn't appreciated enough by the agency's staff, especially its younger employees, so she registered Boss's Day as a holiday with the U.S. Chamber of Commerce. She picked October 16th as the date because it was her father's birthday. Hallmark started selling the cards in 1979, and the rest is history.

When the boss is your father and Boss's Day, not so coincidentally, falls on his birthday by all means celebrate him as much as you like. But don't force it on the rest of us. The unintended consequence of Boss's Day is that it diminishes the boss by obligating subordinates to display gratitude for him, whether genuine or not. If people really want to show their appreciation to the boss, they will gladly do it on their own, sincerely and without any prodding from the boss's daughter or a greeting card company. And no self-respecting boss would want it any other way. I once had a supervisor who eschewed Boss's Day by renaming the holiday "Coworker's Day," and using the opportunity to celebrate all of her staff. Now that's what I'm talking about.

2. Think outside the cubicle. It's vital to know your job, of course, but it's just as important to know your boss's job, too. Gaining a better understanding of the overall operations of your organization, and not just the hows but the whys, has myriad benefits. First, you'll appreciate your work more when you understand how it fits into the larger scheme of things. You'll become a more valuable employee and you'll be better able to provide guidance and assistance to management when called upon.

Ever since 1901 when Ransom Olds put his workers on an assembly line to produce the Oldsmobile Curved Dash, the world's first mass produced car, it's been getting increasingly difficult for employees – especially those of large organizations -to acquire this broader perspective. And it's not just in manufacturing. For white collar work too the trend has continued towards specialization. Jobs have evolved to be narrower for the sake of efficiency, but also in response to the complexity of the modern world.

It takes some effort to overcome the production line culture pervading many workplaces. Aside from asking a lot of questions and maybe doing some research and investigation, for many, the hardest part will be acquiring the mindset required to think beyond their own jobs. Seeing the broader view through their leader's perspective doesn't come naturally for most of us. It requires effort and intention. To get a feel for my boss's perspective, I used to sit in her chair sometimes, briefly, when she was out on vacation, and imagine I was the boss. I had to stop after she returned from a trip to Cancun to find my shoeprints on her desktop.

If you don't know the answers to the following questions, you probably don't know your boss's perspective well enough. What was her journey to becoming the boss? What are the biggest demands her bosses make of her? What's most important to her about the work you're doing? What traits in a colleague does she value most? Is she a dog or cat person? What motivates her? When did she get that teardrop tattoo under her eye? What is her adult beverage of choice? What do those Chinese symbols on her forearm mean?

3. What we have here. A failure to communicate is a failure indeed. There's plenty out there about what to say to your boss and how to say it, but you'll find that a lot of it is missing the point. It's not like a marriage with each side of the communication equation being equal. What your boss communicates is far more important, so you better be paying attention. It's not only what she says, but it's how she says it and when she says it, and what she didn't say. Psychologists believe that 55% of communication is body language, 38% is the tone of your voice, and 7% is the words you speak. If you're hearing just her words, you're missing 93% of the message.

Having regularly scheduled one-on-ones with the boss, even if they're brief, is vital to maintaining a good working relationship. When communicating with the boss, by whatever medium, start off with your main point. Be clear. Be concise. Be direct. Be honest. Be open. Keep your emails to-the-point and avoid the cutesy stuff. Subtlety, nuance, and sarcasm have a place in this world, which is unquestionably *not* in work emails. It's all about the typos and tone. Proofread your emails carefully, then proofread them again before hitting the "Send" button. Proofread them a third time if the button you'll be hitting is "Reply All."

Effective followers are people pleasers at heart, so it can be especially difficult for them to convey disappointing news. But bosses have a way of ferreting out the bad, and it's always better when you can put your spin on it for them. When something goes awry, own up to it. "It's not the crime; it's the cover-up that can get you in real trouble," John Dean, White House counsel, famously advised President Nixon. Admitting that you made a mistake is hard, for a lot of good reasons, but you need to get past it. Give yourself a break. Mistakes are what we humans do. It's actually a refreshing change to hear someone at work readily acknowledge an error and explain the steps taken to ensure that it's not repeated. It's best to communicate bad news in person when you can. Look the boss in the eye and speak clearly. His first reaction might still be anger, but in the long run, your honesty and professionalism will be respected. By me, at least.

4. The boss whisperer. Is working to influence your boss really all that much different from training a horse? Wow, I sure hope so because HR comes down hard on using whips and bridles in professional development exercises. But there is something in the methods of a horse whisperer that's relevant to effective followership. Wiktionary.org defines horse whisperer as,

"A horse trainer who adopts a sympathetic view of the motives, needs, and desires of the horse, based on modern equine psychology." Replace the word "horse" with "boss" in the preceding sentence and you've got a pretty good summation of the concept of effective followership. Effective followers adopt a sympathetic view in order to anticipate and address the boss's needs and wants, moods and predilections for the benefit of all.

What are we? Mind readers? Well, yes. "Perceptive people are always more successful in life and in work," said Loren Miner, COO of the recruitment services company Decision Toolbox and a self-proclaimed expert on reading minds. She believes everyone can develop the ability to mind read, mostly by learning to focus their power of observation. Miner said that the one skill above all others that managers need to be successful is awareness. I believe the same holds true for followers- maybe even more so.

In psychology, the concept is called empathic accuracy and it's a measurement of how well someone can infer the thoughts and feeling of others. People constantly broadcast their thoughts and feelings, but they do it in subtle and abstruse ways. Those with high empathetic accuracy are attuned to the verbal and nonverbal clues people subconsciously exude. They can read into posture, eye movement, voice inflection, and the like. But more importantly, they know how to engage in conversations using empathy and open ended questioning techniques making people more apt to drop the facade and reveal their true feelings. Asking the boss, "So how ya doing today?" is a start. Your follow-up question is really the important one.

5. Grow the f@!% up. When I was a youngster, I saw adults as completely separate and distinct beings from kids -like the two were different lifeforms. Grown-ups were all cigarette smoke, martinis, neckties, instant coffee, and eye shadow. Kids were all PF Flyers, fireflies in a jar, Cap'n Crunch's Crunch Berries, cartoons, and spelling tests. I believed that when people turned a certain age, twenty-one maybe, they magically morphed from one to the other. Yeah, right.

I don't know how to say this in a way that's not going to make you think, "OK boomer," but here goes: If you act like a child at work, you'll be treated like a child at work. Don't think that people don't see it when you're muttering under your breath, rolling your eyes, or playing with your hair. They see it alright, and it annoys the hell out of them. So sit up straight and pay attention in those staff meetings. That's about half of what you're being judged on at work anyway.

You are responsible for your thoughts, your feelings, your actions, your reactions, etc. Taking ownership of your work life means accepting responsibility for it. It means shifting the focus of problems from other people and things onto yourself. It means being accountable. It means being an adult.

While we're on the subject, it couldn't hurt to show some manners in the workplace either. It pains me to have to write this, but common courtesies, which really aren't all that common anymore, must be integral to the modus operandi of effective followers. Or as my grandmother Josie always said to me, "It doesn't cost anything to be kind." Some little things that are actually pretty big things include acknowledging coworkers with a smile and a greeting (e.g. good morning, hello, how are you?), making eye contact when speaking, and standing up when being introduced to someone. Enough said.

CHAPTER 5:

What to Do With a Naked Boss

STEVE JOBS: "Innovation distinguishes
between a leader and a follower."

ME: "Sometimes leaders follow and sometimes
followers lead. All that distinguishes between a leader
and a follower is the moment in time."

It's only in the U.S. that an unalienable right endowed by the Creator is "the pursuit of happiness." With all due respect to Thomas Jefferson and his Declaration of Independence, some of the most miserable folks I've ever met were ones in hot pursuit of happiness. Author and management consultant Tom Rath said, "Scientists are still uncovering the reasons why the pursuit of personal happiness backfires. Part of the explanation lies in its self-focused nature. Research suggests that the more value you place on your own happiness, the more likely you are to feel lonely on a daily basis."

I would add that humans are not designed for happiness. We're designed to survive and reproduce, but being happy doesn't add much in the way of an evolutionary advantage. In fact, natural selection may have disfavored happiness because contented people are more likely to underreact to the things that might threaten their survival. In lieu of happiness, though, evolution gave us something even better: a big brain and with it the analytical abilities for self-reflection, open-mindedness, self-critical thinking, and flexibility so that we can override our own nature's less than helpful tendencies. These are the skills, so essential to the success of any organization, which effective followers nurture. Unfortunately, they are the same ones so lacking in our leaders.

Perhaps you think that I'm being too tough on leaders here, that I should cut them some slack. Well, maybe you're right. Maybe it's not their fault they become pompous, rigid, hard-asses in their climb up the corporate ladder. Research indicates they've been set-up.

Victor Ottati, a professor at Loyola University Chicago, found that people changed, and not in a good way either, after they met with some success. In his 2015 study, two groups of volunteers were administered tests. One group was given an easy test, the other a more difficult one. "Success on these tests puts the person in a position of temporarily feeling that they are an expert," Ottati said, "And then we noticed that the people respond in a more close-minded manner than the people who have recently just failed." Apparently success causes people to become more rigid in their thinking and less willing to consider the views of others. Ottati coined the term "the earned dogmatism effect" for this, and it has been confirmed by other researchers. When you're branded an expert, you begin to feel you've earned the right to disregard others' opinions and to double down on your own views even when presented with evidence to the contrary.

This finding has profound ramifications for how we view leadership and makes perfect sense when you think back on all the supervisors you've worked under in your career. The earned dogmatism effect means that followers, not tainted by the accolades of authority, are better equipped than leaders to determine an organization's course of action in times of change. And we are always in times of change. The ability to be self-critical, self-aware, and self-reflective is powerful – more powerful than expertise. More powerful than intelligence. More powerful than experience. It's even more powerful than data. And there's research that proves it.

The psychologist Philip Tetlock, in his book *Super Forecasting*, argued that when it comes to predicting the future, intelligence, expertise, and information are overrated. He wrote, "A brilliant puzzle-solver may have the raw material for forecasting, but if he doesn't also have an appetite for questioning basic, emotionally charged beliefs, he will often be at a disadvantage relative to a less intelligent person who has a greater capacity for self-critical thinking." It seems implausible that regular folks who practice self-critical thinking and open-mindedness are better than know-it-all experts at predicting the future, but it's true.

In 2011, the Intelligence Advanced Research Projects Activity (IARPA), which is part of the U.S. Office of National Intelligence, proposed a bold experiment. It wanted to know if ordinary citizens, without access to highly classified intelligence information, armed only with their wits, could make better predictions about future geopolitical events than professional experts and analysts who had the government's vast intelligence operations at their disposal. So it held a tournament. Five teams entered the contest, including one organized by Tetlock.

From 2011 to 2015, these teams made predictions on a wide range of topics, from whether voters in Scotland would pass an independence referendum to when Iran would release the *Washington Post*'s Tehran bureau chief, who it had been detaining. It turned out that members of Tetlock's team were very good at forecasting world events. Its top forecasters were 30% better than professional intelligence officers who had access to actual classified information.

One of the best forecasters on Tetlock's team was Elaine Rich, a pharmacist in her 60's from Bethesda, Maryland with no background in international affairs. She signed up for the experiment on a lark, received training in how to estimate probabilities from the team, and then started predicting the future - something she turned out to be eerily good at, placing in the top one percent of the 3,000 forecasters participating in the contest. When asked about her special sources of information, she said, "Usually I just do a Google search."

So how was Tetlock's team of rank amateurs able to beat the experts? The screening of team members played a big part in it. Tetlock chose team members based on the results of an aptitude test he administered to applicants which measured their ability to be open-minded. This turned out to be a huge advantage as the results of the experiment revealed a strong correlation between a team's open-mindedness and the accuracy of its forecasts.

A methodology was applied, too, to maximize the power of this open-mindedness. Team members were taught how to turn their hunches into probabilities. They engaged in online discussions with other members of the team and adjusted their probabilities based on information gleaned from these discussions. This ability to engage in the critical assessment of their own views combined with a willingness to be open to the views of others set members of Tetlock's team apart from the professionals. Additionally, they weren't concerned with protecting their egos or status as experts. "I'm just a pharmacist," Rich said. "Nobody cares about me, nobody knows my name. I don't have a professional reputation at stake. And it's this anonymity which actually gives me freedom to make true forecasts."

The traits which proved so essential to the art of forecasting, ironically, are the same ones diminished by the earned dogmatism effect. Mindset matters. And the mindsets of experts (and bosses) have been groomed to be dogmatic and not conducive to the kind of nimble, open, self-reflective thinking required to forecast the future or guide an organization. The renowned psychologist Carol Dweck found in her extensive research that two fundamental mindsets, fixed and growth, govern people's thoughts and ultimately their actions.

People with a fixed mindset believe that their innate abilities are set in stone. They believe that they either have talent or don't in a particular skill and that's that. Conversely, people with a growth mindset believe that their fundamental qualities are malleable and can be nurtured through their efforts. She writes in her book, *Mindset: The New Psychology of Success*, "The passion for stretching yourself and sticking to it, even (or especially) when it's not going well, is the hallmark of the growth mindset." Not surprisingly,

Dweck found that people with a growth mindset are more likely to be happier and more successful than those with a fixed one.

Implicit in the earned dogmatism effect is the concept that leaders and experts tend to adopt fixed mindsets. They may have started out with a growth mindset, but it's difficult for them to maintain it once they've reached a certain status. Elton John sang "Sorry seems to be the hardest word," but for experts and leaders, the words, "I don't know" are even harder. They don't want their admission that they are still a work in progress, which is fundamental to the growth mindset, to be perceived as weakness. So, to paraphrase Dweck, they become more interested in proving how great they already are than in trying to get better. They hide their deficiencies instead of acknowledging and working on them. They value subordinates who bolster their self-esteem over those who challenge them to grow. They adopt a cut and dried view.

According to Dweck, "Fixed-mindset leaders, like fixed-mindset people in general, live in a world where some people are superior and some are inferior. They must repeatedly affirm that they are superior, and the company is simply a platform for this." Tetlock noted that the best forecasters on his team, aside from being open minded, had a growth mindset, sharing a conviction that predicting the future is a skill that can be nurtured, rather than an inborn aptitude.

When the future isn't what it used to be, leaders can come to be in denial about it, to refuse to see it, even when they're shown a picture of it. That's what happened at Kodak. Founded in 1888 by George Eastman, the company was a dominate force in the photographic film industry for over 100 years. In 2012, however, Kodak filed for bankruptcy and has since sold most of its assets. Its downfall can be traced back to a singular event, an afternoon in late 1975 when its executives failed their Kodak moment. Big time.

On that day, a 26-year-old Kodak engineer, Steve Sasson, proudly presented management with his latest invention: the world's first digital camera. It was as big as a toaster, weighed eight pounds, and its picture quality wasn't great. But there was no denying, at least as far as Sasson was concerned, here was the future of photography. His bosses, however, were nonplussed.

In an interview on YouTube, Sasson talks about his disappointment over their dismissive reaction when shown his digital camera. Leadership focused on its practical downsides, like the difficulty in viewing and storing images given the current state of technology, rather than on its potential. Sasson tried to convince them that the technologies would catch up, but leadership wasn't buying it. Kodak executives could not bring themselves to envision a future without photographic film.

Jeffrey Hayzlett, who was Kodak's chief marketing officer from 2006 until 2010, said in a 2012 interview about the company's demise: "If you want to point back to the most pivotal moment that caused this, it was back in 1975 when they discovered the digital camera and put it back into a closet. Some of the same people are still there. I actually had an executive from Kodak come up to me last week and say, 'I think film's coming back.'"

Aside from this inability to envision the future, another pitfall inherent in a fixed and dogmatic mindset is a susceptibility to the confirmation bias. Confirmation bias is a kind of self-deception where people subconsciously seek out and accept information that supports their own belief systems — and disregard information that throws shade on their opinions. It's the reason fake news is so prevalent and so powerful. We're all guilty of it, but our leaders seem particularly vulnerable to its comforts. The biggest problem with the confirmation bias is that it undermines our ability to have an open mind. Leaders who are so attached to their own opinions that they never want to see or hear any evidence to the contrary are toxic. They may have an open door policy, but if their minds are shut, what good is it?

Awareness of this bias and how it hijacks the decision making process goes a long way to reducing its power. An interesting exercise is to see how often you can recognize it when the confirmation bias pops up in your place of work. Hint: Don't assume you're a divine being when you notice the glut of biases all around you, but none within. It's a lot easier to spot the biases in others than in yourself. But keep digging. I'm sure they're there.

A typical scenario where the confirmation bias comes into play is when the boss excitedly announces her new big idea at a staff meeting. Everyone on the call has at least a half dozen reasons why it's a bad idea immediately pop into their heads, yet nobody wants to be the first to speak up. Instead, everyone keeps thinking, trying to come up with scenarios where the boss's idea might actually work. One of the more senior staff members offers some faint praise, and the rest of the folks around the table fall into line. The marketing researchers and other specialists in the organization know the answer the boss is looking for and then return the data/analysis required to support the initiative. In a nutshell, that's how the world got, albeit only briefly, products such as New Coke, Harley Davidson Perfume, and Colgate Kitchen Entrées.

I call this "the naked emperor syndrome" after the fairy tale *The Emperor's New Clothes* by Hans Christian Anderson. In the story, two sketchy tailors promise to make the emperor a special new suit of clothes. How special? So special, they say, that only smart, competent, well-adjusted, team players can see them. To everyone else, the material will appear invisible. While the tailors act out their charade of assembling the garment, not one of the emperor's coterie admits they actually don't see any fabric. When the emperor parades proudly through town wearing his new "suit", his subjects, too, pretend all is well. The collective delusion is shattered only after a child emerges from the crowd, points to the emperor and starts laughing. "But he isn't wearing anything at all." he says.

I love that kid! He embodies all that's good and decent about effective followership. As an effective follower, sometimes you have to be the one who says the boss is naked. This can be difficult. We evolved as social creatures; we yearn to be accepted. Nobody wants to be labeled a Negative Nelly or heaven forbid, not a team player. Worse yet is devil's advocate, an actual former official position within the Catholic Church for the person tasked with arguing against sainthood for a candidate. Who in their right mind wants to take the opposing view on Saint Bernadette for the Vatican debate team? I've been struck across the knuckles with a ruler for much less, thank you.

It can be downright painful, physically, for the person expressing views that are contrary to those of the group. Gregory Berns, a neuroscientist and author, found that people who dissent from the tribal mentality show heighted activity in the amygdala, the region of the brain's temporal lobes associated with emotional responses. Berns calls this phenomenon "the pain of independence", although I think "the naked emperor syndrome" offers a better description of the experience.

Before you can call out the boss for being naked, though, you have to be able to recognize a naked boss when you see one. (For some of you, this imagery may be disturbing.) You have to think like that kid on the emperor's parade route. I take that back. YOU HAVE TO BE THAT KID. Even though you're a grown up, smarter than most, with twenty years of school and an advanced degree under your belt, with experiences and knowledge and thoughts and ideas (you know stuff), a child sees things that you don't or won't or can't anymore. A child is not afraid of the obvious. An expert may have the best answers, but it's a child who asks the best questions.

There is a concept in Zen Buddhism for this child-like perspective: beginner's mind. It's an attitude of enthusiasm, wonder, and openness, with no preconceived notions when approaching a situation, even one you've encountered many times before. The author of *Zen Mind, Beginner's Mind*, Suzuki Roshi, wrote," If your mind is empty, it is always ready for anything; it is open to everything. In the beginner's mind there are many possibilities; in the expert's mind there are few." That great Buddhist sage from the Motor City and inventor of the Model T, Henry Ford, put it another way: "We have most unfortunately found it necessary to get rid of a man as soon as he thinks himself an expert because no one ever considers himself expert if he really knows his job."

There *are* some simple things you can do to start on the path to a beginner's mind. One is to set an intention every day to be consciously present in the moment. It's simply a matter of being aware and awake at all times rather than operating on autopilot with your thoughts and internal monologue prattling away incessantly in your head. When you're consciously present, you're focusing your attention on the moment-to-moment experiences of life—what's going on around you and what's going on within you. Every relationship, every thought, every gesture will have deeper meaning through the wholehearted attention you bring to it.

Nope, this is not easy. It takes practice, but most of all, it takes intention. Giving yourself a gentle reminder every morning, like when you're looking in the mirror brushing your teeth, to stay in the present moment just for that day can be helpful. I wear a friendship bracelet. I've worn it for so long now that most of the time I don't even think about it. But in moments of uncertainty, when I look down at my hands and see that black and white twine around my left wrist, I am reminded to be mindful. This simple act is surprisingly empowering.

What kind of difference do you think it would make if you could approach each and every workday with a beginner's mind? At the very least, it should make things more interesting- maybe even fun for a change. Once your boss and coworkers got over their initial skepticism, it might even bring you closer to them. With a beginner's mind, you'd have a genuine curiosity about them and their work. You'd be asking more sincere questions and really, really, really listening to their responses. It would definitely spawn some awkward conversations at first, but I'm sure they'd all adjust. What's there not to like? You'd be more open-minded, nonjudgmental, nonthreatening, and appreciative of the opportunities to learn from your workmates. Sounds too good, right?

Try it. Tomorrow morning, before beginning your workday, stand in front of a mirror and take three deep breaths through your nostrils, exhaling slowly each time through your mouth. In your exhales, visualize expelling all those opinions, judgements, notions, expectations, criticisms, and over-thinking about work. Watch them leave your body, floating out, dissipating in a cloud. You should immediately feel more relaxed in your shoulders; it takes a lot of tension to carry that stuff around all day. Dropping all the institutional baggage of how things are supposed to be will help you to see things for how they could be. And should be. So the next time the boss parades around the office naked you'll be able to tell him, "Hey. Go put on a robe."

CHAPTER 6:

The Follower Manifesto

BOB DYLAN: "You're gonna have to serve somebody."

ME: "Well then it might as well be for a good and just cause."

If you're working out of necessity for an organization with a less than admirable purpose, don't feel too bad. I get it. You can't buy groceries with your good looks alone, although I've never actually tried and am just assuming that the ten-item-or-less lane at the StopNShop doesn't work that way. Most employees are only in it for a paycheck. Take that away and workplace attendance drops precipitously- especially on the Monday after Super Bowl.

But it can't be only about the Benjamins. Money gets employees through the door, but it won't engage them. I know what you're thinking: "If I only made [pick a number, any number] more dollars a week, I'd be a lot happier at work." But trust me or better yet, trust the research on this, the money won't make you happier. The studies are clear. The association between salary and job satisfaction is very weak. Or in the words of The Notorious B.I.G., "Mo' money, mo' problems."

The more we make, the more we want. Isn't that just being greedy? Yes, but from the standpoint of an evolutionary biologist (and Gordon Gekko), greed is good. Biologically speaking, for any organism to be successful it has to be more than a little greedy. And there haven't been too many species more successful than Homo sapiens over the last 40,000 years. Our greed is baked in.

That cave couple who kept stockpiling firewood even after all their friends and neighbors long since stopped survived the worst winter in a millennium. Their contented neighbors froze to death while they were able to stay warm enough to pass on their greedy genes to their children who passed them on to their children and so on until they eventually made it to you. (That's right. You're going around in your ancestor's old greedy genes and not just on casual Fridays.) As a species, we are hardwired for dissatisfaction.

It's been said that people never seem to get enough of what they don't want. Indeed, the more we have, the less effective it is at bringing us joy. Dan Gilbert, a Harvard psychology professor notes, "Once you get basic human needs met, a lot more money doesn't make a lot more happiness." Here's why: Money won't make you like yourself any more than you do. Let that sink in for a moment. Money won't make you like yourself any more than you do.

People have come to believe it's a luxury, or at the very least an afterthought, to be working for an organization whose values echo their own when shouldn't this be the prime consideration when job hunting? For most of us in the real world, however, there are too many practical matters to consider (e.g. salary, location, opportunity for advancement, are they even going to offer me the job?) before the organization's mission figures into the decision. But what if people didn't have to choose between their values and those of their employer? Perhaps they don't anymore.

Employees, consumers, and citizens are now demanding that companies behave more ethically, and companies are responding in a positive manner. They can't afford not to. In addition to turning a profit, companies are now expected to be responsible citizens of the global community. Their advertising promotes their civic achievements as much as their products. Leadership has been put on notice, thanks in part to the #MeToo movement. CEOs behaving badly are pilloried on social media and expose their organizations to tremendous public backlash. And why not? In the *Citizens United* and *Hobby Lobby* cases, the Supreme Court affirmed that corporations are people. If that's the case, then they ought to be people we'd want as friends because as consumers we've brought them into our homes where they're ingratiating themselves with our families.

Followers are finding new and different ways to influence their organization's karmic footprints. In August of 2019, political activist employees at Google circulated a petition demanding that their company not do business with U.S. Customs and Border Protection. This was in response to news reports that the agency was separating migrant children from their parents after illegal border crossings and holding the children in cages. The petition actually referenced Nazis and made clear that Google employees, unlike those of the Third Reich, were not going to be just following orders. It read in part, "We have only to look to IBM's role working with the Nazis during the Holocaust to understand the role that technology can play in automating mass atrocity. History is clear: the time to say NO is now. We refuse to be complicit." It was quickly signed by nearly 1,500 Google employees.

Not so coincidentally, later that same month, Google banned political discussions among its employees at work. Its new policy instructed employees to "avoid controversies that are disruptive to the workplace and that make fellow employees feel like they don't belong. " It goes on to read, "While sharing information and ideas with colleagues helps build community, disrupting the workday to have a raging debate over politics or the latest news story does not."

It's a bit ironic that Google of all companies (whose original corporate motto was "Don't be evil") is dictating what its employees can discuss in the workplace. After all Google, which made it easier to access the information, disinformation and misinformation bolstering our own worldviews, is part of what's fueling these raging debates in the first place. But I suspect it's not the debates themselves that worry Google. It's their lack of civility, which correlates directly with the rise of social media. But not for effective followers; we're nothing if not civil.

Employees of other companies, too, did not want any part of the immigration controversy. Whole Foods employees demanded that its parent company stop doing business with a government contractor that was singled out for working with Immigration and Customs Enforcement (ICE). Wayfair employees protested when the company provided the furnishings for an immigration detention camp. There was a near mutiny among employees at Oglivy, a PR agency that developed an ad campaign to recruit employees for U.S. Customs and Border Protection. So far, political activism among employees hasn't had much success in changing companies, but it's not going away.

A 2019 survey conducted by the website *Quartz at Work* found that a surprising 38% of respondents reported that they've spoken out in support of or to criticize their employer regarding a public issue. Move over boomers. Millennials, people born from 1981 to 1996, are most likely to self-identify as employee activists; baby boomers, born from 1946 to 1964, are the least. Millennials are also the most likely employees to believe it's justified to call out their employers over their handling of controversial issues.

Employees of technology firms recently began taking a novel approach to influencing management at their companies: exercising their rights as shareholders. For tech start-ups and established firms like Amazon, Google, and Facebook, stock has always been an essential component of the employee compensation package. Like any other stockholder, employees at these firms have the right to bring forward shareholder proposals, and for the first time, workers are doing just that.

In 2018, more than a dozen Amazon employees filed shareholder petitions asking the company to develop a plan to address its effect on climate change. Google employees pushed for a proposal at its shareholder meeting to link executive pay to corporate diversity and inclusion. This approach ultimately may be more about throwing shade at company founders than garnering a majority of votes at shareholder meetings. It's hard to outvote the founder when he owns most of the voting stock. Jeff Bezos, Amazon's founder and largest shareholder, owns 16 percent of the company; Google's founders, Larry Page and Sergey Brin, control 56 percent of the voting shares of its parent company. Still, the publicity these campaigns generate can be an effective motivator for company leaders, who are especially sensitive to public scorn.

If you're not a political activist or high-flying techie with stock options to leverage, don't despair. There's another way to cast aspersions on your company- by harnessing all the public shaming power of social media. In 2014, Kristie Williams, a 25-year-old Starbucks barista in Atlanta, started an online petition through the website Coworker.org calling for Starbucks to change its dress code policy to allow visible tattoos. It's hard to believe, but at that time the mocha-java giant made its employees cover their body tattoos at work. (And you thought tattoos were mandatory for employment there.)

Williams has a tattoo of her daughter's name, Summer Blythe, written in elegant script on her left forearm. She had to wear long-sleeved shirts at work -even when the store's air conditioning conked out and even though long sleeves on a barista quickly become soaked in coffee gunk. The petition quickly garnered over 25,000 signatures, with many of the signatories expressing outrage that their favorite coffee shop would stifle the free expression of body art.

In addition, Williams encouraged her fellow employees to share photos of their uncovered tattoos on Instagram with the hashtags #sbuxtattoos and #tobeapartner. Within months, Starbucks relented and changed its tattoo policy to be more reasonable. It's so reasonable that it ought to be everyone's personal tattoo policy: "Tattoos are allowed, but not on your face or throat. Treat tattoos as you treat speech – you can't swear, make hateful comments or lewd jokes in the workplace, neither can your tattoos."

Coworker.org has facilitated many other successful campaigns since this one, some involving serious worker's rights issues. A noteworthy example is that a tipping option was added to the Uber app in 2017 in response to a Coworker.org campaign. Companies like Starbucks, who care about their hipster-cred and whose workforces include a fair share of millennials, appear to be especially susceptible to these kinds of campaigns. For employees who want to influence their company's policies but aren't unionized, these online platforms may be the closest they'll ever get to collective bargaining. As the expectations and awareness of consumers rise, social media campaigns ultimately may prove to be a more effective means than collective bargaining for employees to influence company management. Social media and the crowdsourcing of grievances could turn out to be the labor unions of the twenty-first century.

There can be a downside for the employees behind these campaigns. Frankly, employers don't like to be publicly shamed by their employees on social media. Their colleagues, too, often don't appreciate the tension and conflict these disputes bring to the workplace. In most cases, it's illegal to fire or retaliate against employees who join together in an effort to improve their working conditions. But that doesn't stop the Coworker.org website from warning potential users, "Anyone who starts a campaign on Coworker.org risks getting fired or facing some sort of retaliation from a supervisor."

I can't stress enough how fundamental it is to the concept of effective followership to work for an organization whose vision, mission, and values align with your own. (This is especially true if you're self-employed.) People experience greater fulfillment when they live and work in accordance with their values. When we don't honor our values, we suffer. It's as simple as that.

The biggest obstacle people face to living a life that's true to them is the fact that they've never actually identified what it is that's true to them. They've never gained a clear understanding of what their own deepest values are. How could they? This isn't taught in schools. Religious organizations are quick to tell you what their values are, but I don't think they're especially interested in hearing about yours- at least none of the groups I've been associated with ever asked me my views on transubstantiation.

We're now entering the part of our journey that's going to take some effort. Stop. Don't turn the page. Come back here. It's just a little bit of effort, but there's a huge reward. I guarantee it. One of the best ways to identify what's important to you is through the act of writing. Writing is the single most important part of the self-discovery process. There's no way around it. Even if you've never written anything before, you have to do this. It's easier than you think.

Write a personal manifesto. I know the word "manifesto" conjures up images of a bushy bearded communist or the Unabomber, who was eventually caught when his brother, recognizing his writing style after he demanded that his manifesto be published in newspapers, reported him to the FBI. Simply put, a manifesto is a declaration of beliefs, core values, ideals, and intentions. According to The Art of Manliness website, "A manifesto functions as both a statement of principles and a bold, sometimes rebellious, call to action. By causing people to evaluate the gap between those principles and their current reality, the manifesto challenges assumptions, fosters commitment, and provokes change."

There's no right or wrong format for a personal manifesto; the important thing is to just write one. A good way to start is to type "I believe…" at the top of a page, then start listing things you feel strongly about, things that are important to you, things you want to be remembered for. On another page, write "I want to…" and then list the actions you want to take to improve the world. If you're still not sure how to get started, look online at some examples. But don't make all of their beliefs, values, and actions your own. It's still *your* personal manifesto.

So what do you do with this thing after it's written? The short answer is, "Live it." Read your manifesto regularly to reaffirm its values and remind you of your goals. Maintaining it in the forefront of your mind will have a subtle yet profound impact on your actions. Keep it handy. Print it and hang it up in your workspace. Place a copy in an inconspicuous place in your home. Your manifesto will always be a work in progress (like you). It's a document to be referred to and revised often.

Armed with your newly found self-knowledge, you can assess the merits of your current workplace. If you've been there for more than three days, you probably already know the answers to these questions, but ask them of yourself anyway. Is this organization and its leadership worthy of my followership? Do their values align with and support my own? Do I like it here? Does the organization's mission make the world a better place? And finally, does it pay my bills? A no answer to any of these questions means that it's time to move on.

And it isn't all about the organization either. Even if you're working for a superb organization, with ethical leadership, creating happiness in others (sign me up for that) you must be aware of the implications and consequences of your attitudes and actions at work. Moving to a new organization doesn't make things any better when you're the problem. No matter where you go, there you are.

Again, you probably already know the answers to these questions, but ask them of yourself anyway. Am I that guy at work? You know, that guy? Do people take a deep breath and sigh before asking me to do something, like my job, at work? Is it mom and dad's fault I'm not an astronaut? A yes answer to any of these questions means that your company might not be the problem here.

Working a job, especially one that's not fulfilling, can be physically and emotionally exhausting. It doesn't leave much time or energy to look for a more rewarding one. But that's no excuse to stay where you are. Changing jobs is scary, but scary can be a good thing. Embrace the scary. After all, you owe it to yourself to work for a place that deserves you. Companies with authentic values that are consistent with those of its employees are just better places to be. When we put our values front and center in our work lives, it's incredibly invigorating. When we don't, it's draining. Those of you reading this while plopped down on the couch after another one of those days at work know exactly what I mean.

It can be hard to get a sense of an organization's work climate from the interview and application process, so it pays to do some research on your prospective new employers. Probably the best way to find what you're look-ing for is to ask around. Check LinkedIn to see if anyone you know currently works or previously worked for that organization. Ask them about the cor-porate climate. An organization's values set the tone for its climate.

The actual job itself matters, too. It's amazing to think how little the workplace has changed in the 2,500 years since the Buddha first taught his philosophy for earning a living. Teacher, farmer, cab driver (the ancient Romans invented the taxi meter), construction worker, and tax accoun-tant, to name just a few, have remained standard occupations through the millennia. Right Livelihood is probably the most important but least dis-cussed of the eight parts of the path to overcoming suffering laid out by the Buddha. It covers where we work, what we do, and how we do it. According to Zen teacher Thich Nhat Hanh, "To practice Right Livelihood, you have to find a way to earn your living without transgressing your ideals of love and compassion." Since you've already written a personal manifesto, you know exactly what those ideals are. If your life's work doesn't support them, maybe a change is in order.

Effective followership ultimately comes down to supporting the noble mission of the organization; performing work that brings joy; and performing it with integrity in an ethical manner. Notice what effective followership is *not* about? Leaders.

CHAPTER 7:

Bad Bosses in the Midst

VINCE LOMBARDI: "Leaders are made; they are not born."

ME: "They're made by followers, who are usually
the ones doing all the actual work."

For the typical leader, his ego is a delicate thing, requiring meticulous care and cultivation and plenty of fertilizer. It's sort of like an orchid- a giant, hideous, flesh-eating orchid.

According to Sigmund Freud, ego is one of the three parts of the psyche, along with the id and super-ego. The ego is the organized, realistic part that mediates between the desires of the id and the desires of the super-ego. Ego is that thing in our consciousness that tricks us into thinking we're separate, that we are an entity distinct from our environment and those populating it. And we're not. It's an illusion. It's all an illusion.

Even if you're not open to the concept, you have to admit that there have been times in your life when you've experienced glimpses of this interconnectedness, this oneness with everything. Maybe it was a time you sat silently in awe of a brilliant sunset or when you held your child for the first time. In these brief moments, you knew that you were connected to everything and that everything is going to be all right. Unfortunately, these moments are so few and far between that we spend most of our days shrouded in the illusion of separateness.

Once people buy into the notion that they're apart from others, it's just a short ideological hop to believing that they're better (or in some cases worse) than others. And the rest of their days are spent proving to the world and themselves that they are worthy of that opinion. Or worthy of love. Worthy of happiness. Worthy of a second chance. Yep, these are the world's great leaders: inspired by ego, driven by self-importance. And the whole while, paraphrasing an old Indian-American aphorism of Deepak Chopra, their self-importance is just a mask for self-pity.

Of course there are leaders who aren't driven by self-importance. But this doesn't necessarily mean that they're good leaders. Many of them are "accidental leaders." These are people who were the best mechanics in the shop and because of that skill now find themselves managing the dealership's service department. They got into their career because of a love of cars and soon discover that overhauling an automatic transmission on an Acura requires a completely different set of socket wrenches than reprimanding the new service tech who forgot to tighten an oil drain plug. But that doesn't stop organizations from forcing people into making that giant leap from great worker to lousy boss. And there's not a leadership seminar in the world that can replace a love of automobiles with a love of middle management. These leaders didn't start out as ego driven, but they usually end up that way. Insecurity corrupts and absolute insecurity corrupts absolutely.

There are things you can do right now to help dispel the illusion of separateness (that don't involve renouncing your Netflix account or joining a monastery.) Practicing mindfulness is a good one. There are many excellent resources available on mindfulness, so I won't delve too deeply into the subject here. In a nutshell, I'd say that mindfulness is the practice of returning again and again to the present moment.

Seeing through the illusion of separateness is important because it helps in the cultivation of empathy, but it's not a prerequisite for empathy. I have known some incredibly empathetic people who have never picked up a new-age book in their lives. Yet somewhere along the way they acquired the ability to put themselves in the shoes of others. For those of us who aren't as blessed, it's going to take some practice. Once you can recognize that even that condescending jerk in your office, who continually belittles you for no apparent reason, shares with you the same spark, that same divine light, she no longer has power over you. Once you empathize with her, she's no longer just that bully from work. She's becomes a person, one with whom you probably share a lot more in common than you'd like to admit.

In order to fully support your organization's mission, you're going to have to learn to empathize with its leaders, customers, and your fellow followers. Empathy is not kindness. It is not pity. It's the ability to see the divine in everyone, including yourself. People who are good empathizers (surely you must know some) consider things from perspectives other than their own. They are able to appreciate how others must feel and apply that understanding to their interactions with them.

Quick tips for cultivating empathy:

1. Mindfulness matters. Engage in mindfulness to diminish the perception of separateness. There are plenty of resources out there on the practice, but Vietnamese monk Thich Nhat Hanh, who was one of the West's first teachers of mindfulness, is still one of the best.

2. Pay attention. Give the people in your life the attention they deserve. BTW-This is also one of the best ways to ensure you get their attention.

3. Your undivided attention, please. For God's sake, put down that iPhone when people are talking with you. You can't multitask. Nobody can. If we could there wouldn't be so many cars wrapped around telephone poles (or worse) because the driver was texting.

4. A sense of curiosity. Research has shown that being an open, curious person leads to better interpersonal relationships. People who are curious are just more fun to be around. And they're good empathizers because they ask the kinds of questions that give them a better understanding of peoples' experiences and points of view.

5. Be genuine. Unless you're creepy. In that case, reign in the creepiness and fake being genuine.

Consultants are pushing companies to improve their "customer experience" as a way to distinguish themselves from their competition. They offer professional development in human relations and other soft skills intended to improve the quality of service offered to customers. It's all a big fat waste. If they're not built on a foundation of empathy, they're just empty skills like wiggling your ears or riding a unicycle. Empathy isn't a skillset; it's a mindset. Empathic people don't have to think about what skills to apply when working with customers. Helpfulness flows naturally from them.

Flight attendants were once the embodiment of customer service, back in the time when passengers dressed up for flying. Those days are gone. Remember that viral video from 2017 of an incident on a United Airlines plane? The flight crew was fully trained in the customer experience. Yet, they stood by and watched as security dragged a 69-year-old passenger by the arms down the center aisle and off the plane. He was a doctor who refused to give up his seat to a United Airlines employee because he had patients he needed to see the next morning, and this was the last flight of the day.

The supervisor and flight crew did nothing wrong, according to airline CEO Oscar Munoz. He said, "Our employees followed established procedures for dealing with situations like this. While I deeply regret this situation arose, I also emphatically stand behind all of you, and I want to commend you for continuing to go above and beyond to ensure we fly right." Huh? The CEO's message to employees here seems to be "Our procedures are more important to us than our customers."

We train employees what to do, but just as important is how they do it. In this case, although the employees followed procedures to the letter, the results were a public relations nightmare. Why? Because they were hollow followers, who showed little empathy for the passengers who were about to be bumped late on a Sunday night with the next available flight not until Monday afternoon. Their attitudes stunk from the get-go. Passengers reported that right after the plane boarded, an airline representative in a belligerent tone announced over the intercom, "We have United employees that need to fly to Louisville tonight. And this flight's not leaving until four people get off." At that point, I wouldn't have voluntarily left the plane either.

They might as well have had Bette Davis announce, "Fasten your seatbelts; it's going to be a bumpy night."

Organizations don't value and promote empathy among their employees because, quite frankly, their leaders just don't get it. A 2013 study published in the journal *Personnel Psychology* found that narcissists are more likely than modest people to attain positions of leadership. (No kidding.) And what's a fundamental characteristic of narcissism? A lack of empathy, of course. Narcissists, among their other crappy tendencies, can't feel or appreciate the feelings of others.

The Mayo Clinic defines narcissistic personality disorder (NPD) as "a mental condition in which people have an inflated sense of their own importance, a deep need for excessive attention and admiration, troubled relationships, and a lack of empathy for others. But behind this mask of extreme confidence lies a fragile self-esteem that's vulnerable to the slightest criticism." Sound like someone you know? Sound a little like everyone you know?

We all have a little narcissist in us. I've yet to meet someone who didn't behave as if they were the most important person in their own life. (Although, to be fair, I haven't met the Dalai Lama and moms can be pretty selfless.) Leaders tend to be on the extreme side of the narcissist scale; effective followers on the near side. Do narcissists make good leaders? Dr. Emily Grijalva, the lead author of the Personnel Psychology study and a noted narcissism expert, stated, "Our findings are pretty clear that the answer to the question as to whether narcissism is good or bad is that it is neither. It's best in moderation."

Extreme narcissists create workplace atmospheres that are noxious, chaotic, and stressful on those around them. This is because where everybody else suffers, narcissists thrive. In difficult work environments and in difficult times, lack of empathy can actually be a strength. Narcissist leaders find it easier than others to make those tough work decisions to eliminate jobs, close facilities, or lay-off employees. For the follower, navigating successfully through their world is difficult, but it can be done. To paraphrase Dr. Grijalva, it all comes down to the right mix of kick ass and kiss ass.

She said, "There might be a trade-off between narcissistic leaders' needing a subordinate who is confident enough to earn the leader's respect, but also deferential enough to show the leader unwavering admiration." For the effective follower, it's a constant balancing act. They exude what's best described as "non-threatening competence." They are super cognizant of how of their words and deeds are perceived or might be misconstrued. And they carefully consider the consequences before acting or speaking. Anything less with a narcissist is done at their own peril.

Here's a little cautionary tale about a narcissist from my own career:

On a Monday, my supervisor stepped into my office and shut the door behind him. It seems that his boss, the deputy superintendent, wanted an analysis conducted of a major department in our organization. He wanted a report on its functions, structure, work flow, etc. and recommendations on how the department could improve its efficiency. She had already told the department's managers that I would be reviewing their operations and that she expects complete cooperation from their leadership and staff. Oh, and the finished report must be on her desk by Friday before noon.

A project that normally would take four weeks had to be completed in four days. I worked dutifully that week, interviewing managers and employees, reviewing work flow charts, job descriptions, and other data. My findings and recommendations were assembled into a nice neat, concise report. I left the office at 1:30 am on Friday after placing a copy of the report on my supervisor's desk with a sticky note: "I'd like to proofread this once more in the morning with a fresh set of eyes before it's given to the deputy superintendent."

Shortly after arriving at work the next morning, my supervisor's administrative assistant called, saying that my supervisor wanted to see me right away. I was exhausted, but feeling proud as I walked down the hall toward his office. "What's this about needing to proofread it again?" he said as I stepped through his doorway. "Don't ever put anything on my desk unless it's perfect." He tossed my report at me and it landed on the floor.

I was literally crestfallen. Standing there in his office, I could feel my chest deflate and my body slump forward. "I will never be perfect," I said.

"I'm human. No matter how careful and conscientious I am, the best I'll ever be is fallible." (I'd learned these lines from a book about perfectionists and repeated them to myself often.) If only I had stopped there. If only.

Fueled by fatigue and self-righteousness, I continued. "I can't believe you called me in here to bust my chops. You're the worst boss I've ever had." My supervisor immediately softened his stance. He told me that the report looked good and that I should deliver it personally to the deputy superintendent, who was always so appreciative of my work here. But the damage was done.

Nobody likes to be told they're the worst ever; narcissists hate it. My supervisor surrounded himself with glad handers and yes men- which, from that point on, decidedly did not include me. We worked together for five years after that, and I always felt like I was on the outside looking in. On good days, he viewed me with suspicion, on bad days as an enemy. I tried, but nothing could erase that moment. Telling your supervisor he's the worst boss ever? Spoiler alert! Not a good career move.

Taylor Swift so eloquently asked the musical question we've all wondered on occasion about a boss: "Why ya gotta be so mean?" It could be because he's insecure. Remember how prevalent the imposter syndrome is among the powerful? (And people think followers are the insecure ones. As if.) Research shows that leaders who are insecure in their jobs tend to be tougher on their subordinates. Threatened self-esteem spawns aggression. So why do leaders continue to get away with this rude behavior? Because it works. Experiments have shown that people perceive someone who is harshly negative to be smarter than someone who gives positive feedback.

A 2016 Michigan State University study, reported in the *Journal of Applied Psychology*, found that employees subjected to such rude behavior get worn down over time, and as a result have a tendency to act in a similar manner. Russell Johnson, coauthor of the study, said, "This mental fatigue, in turn, led them to act uncivil toward other workers. In other words, they paid the incivility forward." And that's how a workplace becomes toxic.

Insecure leaders are the pits. At least with a narcissist you know what you're getting day in and day out (a self-centered jerk-face), and you can plan accordingly. The unhinged personality swings of an insecure boss can be a real challenge. If it's a good day and he's feeling confident, effective followers behave accordingly, right up until that moment when a stray comment from a less enlightened subordinate triggers the leader's insecurity. He suddenly becomes defensive, vindictive, petty, and mean. Have a nice day.

Quick tips for dealing with an insecure boss:

1. **The compassion reaction**. Maintain an empathetic mindset. Haven't we all been in an insecure place at one time or another? It's not easy being the boss. Sympathy, compassion, and understanding will help you respond to your workplace with grace and prevent you from dehumanizing that rotten, stinking, no good excuse for a shift supervisor who is making your life miserable.

2. **Focus on the work.** Work hard without fanfare to make your organization successful. Working quietly behind the scenes has its own rewards. You don't need approval or recognition from your boss for a job well done. She's not your mom. And work is not an elementary school piano recital.

3. **Don't dish the dirt.** Keep busy, too busy for those coworker-led bitch sessions. They won't make you feel any better and these conversations have a way of getting back to the boss. If you really need to vent about the boss, bend the ear of your partner or a good friend. Warning: A little of this kind of talk is a lot. Let it out and move on quickly to a more mutually interesting subject.

4. **Be transparent.** Hide nothing and have nothing to hide. Insecure managers fear the unknown and assume the unintended. Transparency goes a long way toward gaining their trust.

Some of you are thinking, "Insecure boss? Ha! I'd take that over my boss any day of the week." A boss so confident that he thinks he can do anybody's job better than they're doing it, from the managers to the receptionist to the sales team, and more than happy to let everybody know about it, isn't a whole lot of fun either. Yet there are times when effective followers relish and even seek out the opportunity to work under such tyrannical leaders.

Steve Jobs, who died in 2011, was co-founder and CEO of Apple and a pioneer in the nascent personal computing industry of the 1970s. He was forced out in 1985, but returned to Apple in 1997 to lead it from the brink of bankruptcy to become the most valuable company in the world at one time. By all accounts, Jobs was a horrible boss: abusive, abrasive, and aggressive. He was a perfectionist who demanded nothing less than perfection from all his employees. Yet he was able to garner the devotion and admiration of a good many of them.

There was a story told at Apple about an intern who once shared an elevator ride with Jobs in the company's headquarters. When Jobs asked the intern about what he was working on and the intern didn't give a clear enough answer he was fired by Jobs by the time he reached his floor. The tale may be apocryphal, but that didn't stop employees at Apple from avoiding the elevator altogether or always having something engaging in mind to say to the boss just in case they found themselves in that same situation.

Andrea Cunningham, who worked with Jobs in the marketing of Apple's original Macintosh, said of her former employer, "Steve got angry with everybody that worked with him. He was very impatient. He had a vision of what it was that you were supposed to be accomplishing and if you didn't do it fast enough or you didn't do it right enough, he definitely got angry. He threw things at people, nothing heavy, but he threw wads of paper at people, swore at people, criticized their clothing. He did all those things."

Jobs unceremoniously fired Cunningham, and she had to threaten him with going to the press in order to be paid $35,000 still owed to her by Apple. Jobs then offered to hire her back, and Cunningham accepted, even following him to his other ventures with NeXT and Pixar. Guy Kawasaki was an engineer at Apple and wrote of his experiences, "I worked at Apple from 1983 to 1987, and then from 1995 to 1997. Although I refer to these stints as 'two tours of duty,' it was a privilege and an honor to work there. In many ways, I am who I am and where I am because of Steve Jobs and Apple." But did Kawasaki enjoy working for him? "IMHO, the question is framed wrong", he wrote. "You're not necessarily supposed to 'enjoy' working for someone. That's why work is called work, not play."

Cunningham, Kawasaki, and the others who stayed and remained loyal to Jobs did so because the potential upside of working with him was so great. Jobs and his followers were in essence using each other to achieve goals that were mostly compatible- but not entirely so. For the followers, there was the prestige of Apple, the résumé building, the opportunity to learn and hone new skills, the money, of course, and the excitement of developing cutting edge products like the iPhone. For Jobs, there was the products.

When Jobs returned to Apple for his second stint in 1997, he called the company's top employees together and asked them to tell him "what's wrong with this place." After listening to several unsatisfying responses, he prodded the group by saying, "It's the products. So what's wrong with the products?" After no clear responses again, Jobs finally shouted at them, "The products *suck!*"

Jobs is quoted as saying, "If you keep your eye on the profit, you're going to skimp on the product. But if you focus on making really great products, then the profits will follow." And true to his word, that's what Jobs focused on, at the expense of all else, especially his employees. But they knew that, and for the ones who could put up with it, it didn't matter. They weren't there to be part of a family. They were in it for themselves.

Quick tips for working for a tyrant.

1. If you are going to put up with that nonsense, it better be worth it. Like the Apple employees, make sure that you're getting more out of your followership than the boss is getting from his leadership. Steve Jobs could get away with that egregious behavior because he was a genius with a proven track record of crazy success and for making those under him successful, too. Your ill-mannered, overbearing excuse for a crew chief probably doesn't have that going for him so it should be readily apparent to you what the benefits of working for him actually are. (Which should be significant.) "My job is not to be easy on people. My job is to make them better," Jobs said. If your boss isn't making you better, it might be time to move on.

2. Embrace your inner sociopath. Recognize your boss for what she is. If you're working for a bully, don't be shocked when she acts like a bully.

And don't take it personally either. It's just business. As an effective follower, you are in control of the situation and your emotions. Keep reminding yourself of why you're working there in the first place. And it's not for the boss's sake.

3. The best policy. Be honest with the boss. That's what Guy Kawasaki took as a life lesson from his time working under Jobs. "The wiser the person, the more they yearn for the truth," he wrote. My father's sage advice on this topic was in a similar vein. "Son," he said, "never BS a BSer."

Whether you find yourself working for a narcissistic leader, an insecure one, or a tyrant the strategies of effective followership are the same. You don't have to quit your job. If it's a good, sound organization and you liked it there before Godzilla arrived, by all means, stay. It's likely that you can outlast him- even triumph. Managers typically stay in a job for only two to three years, and crummy ones tend to flame out even sooner. The trick to prevailing in these situations is to keep the focus on yourself.

"Keep the focus on yourself." I first heard those words of wisdom over thirty years ago when I was working as a housing inspector for the local municipality. It was bestowed upon me by a fellow inspector, a cantankerous gentleman named Mitchell (not his real name), who said it to anyone within earshot. And everyone was within earshot in that office. The inspectors' desks, all eight of them, were in a single room. No cubicles. Every word uttered by one could be heard by all. I can attest to this.

In my first week on the job, I returned from my morning rounds to find a note on my desk to return a phone call from a Mr. Lyon. I dialed the number, and a woman's voice answered "Maryland Zoo, how can I help you?" I had hardly finished saying, "May I speak with Mr. Lyon" before the entire room erupted in laughter. And I don't think they were laughing *with* me.

Whenever Mitchell overheard someone complain about a coworker, the boss, the bureaucrats in the commissioner's office, housing court judges, or anyone else for that matter, he would growl, "Keep the focus on yourself." This certainly had a chilling effect on those conversations, which soon became restricted to the lavatory stalls. His refrain shortened to "Keep the focus" before eventually he just shouted a single word at people engaged in negative speech. "Focus."

Mitchell had no patience for the ersatz office drama these conversations stirred up. He was a troubled man, with a life so filled with real drama (recovery, relapse, garnished wages, ex-wives, child support, etc.) that there wasn't room for the faux office kind. This is the antithesis of the lousy leader, who uses drama the same way an octopus uses ink. (The difference being that the octopus has more backbone.)

Your best defense when you find yourself working for a horrible boss is to work hard and work quietly. Remind yourself that you don't need to be recognized for your efforts. As Ralph Waldo Emerson said, "The reward of a thing well done is having done it." If your office has a grindstone, put your nose to it.

Your colleagues are going to want to commiserate with you. Don't. Channel the spirit of Mitchell and keep the workplace chatter productive. It's not a Victorian melodrama or a sci-fi epic. You are not the victim (or hero) here. Your boss is not an evil cyborg bent on destroying the planet. It's work. Just work. Remember, lousy leaders love the drama. Don't give them the satisfaction.

Although effective followers aren't in it for the accolades, a little acknowledgment of our contributions every now and then would be nice. We are human after all. Sometimes in order to get recognition, you have to give recognition. Wait for a situation to arise in which your leader has truly managed you well. For more than a few of you, this is going to require some patience. Then let her know it. Caveat alert: the complement must be genuine. Anything less comes across as phony and manipulating, which of course it is.

Leaders eat it up when employees tell them how they were able to resolve a difficult work problem through the incisive application of their guidance and wisdom. I haven't met a leader yet who didn't puff up a little after being told by a subordinate how great they are. And if that leader has a shred of common decency, she will return the compliment at the next opportunity.

As an added bonus, what you say about others influences how they view you. Gretchen Rubin, author of the book, *The Happiness Project*, found that people associate you with the qualities that you ascribe to them. When you compliment a coworker for being trustworthy and caring, she will be inclined to think of you in those terms, too. Warning: This works the same for criticism. If you are constantly knocking your coworkers for being petty and spiteful, those negative qualities will become associated with you as well. This was expressed to me this way on the Stoneleigh Elementary School playground, "I'm rubber and you're glue. Whatever you say bounces off me and sticks to you."

It is possible to toot your own horn without being too obnoxious. The key: show, don't tell. As the old-school gospel duo Iola and Sullivan Pugh sang: "May the work I've done speak for me! / When I'm resting in my grave/ There is nothing that can be said/ May the work I've done speak for me!" (Check them out on YouTube. Their harmonies give me chills.)

CHAPTER 8:

Smithers Versus the Springfield Nuclear Power Plant Disaster

ALEXANDER GRAHAM BELL: "Mr. Watson. Come here.
I want to see you." [First words over a telephone.]

ME: Would ♥ 2 but after 5. Already punched out. ☹
[Text message reply.]

Can a cartoon character personify something? If so, there are few people, animated or not, who embody bad followership any better than Waylon J. Smithers, a.k.a. Mr. Smithers, a.k.a. Smithers. (Can't you just hear the voice of Mr. Burns when you read that name?) Smithers is the sycophantic assistant to Charles Montgomery Burns, owner of the Springfield Nuclear Power Plant on the long-running television show *The Simpsons*. He's the quintessential cliché of a bad follower, and unfortunately for many people, the image that comes to mind when they think of followership.

Smithers is a toady, driven to do just about anything, ethical or not, by his obsessive need for the approval of Mr. Burns. His blind loyalty to a greedy, evil leader and to an organization that decidedly does not make Springfield a better place, causes even sheep to look down their noses at him. I know he's just a fictional character on a satirical, animated TV sitcom, but I really dislike the guy. (In his defense, he could borrow a line from a fellow cartoon character, Jessica Rabbit, who notably said, "I'm not bad. I'm just drawn that way.") Smithers' brand of followership is the stereotype I'm trying to overcome, and it lends its name to one of the three types of followers (Smithers, Hollow, and Effective) I've identified through my years in the workplace.

The Smithers-es of the world are scary and dangerous and not a whole lot of fun to vacation with. These are the people in the workplace who are drawn to charismatic and powerful leaders by a deep-seated need either for their approval or a paycheck. If it's the former, heaven help them. If it's the latter, welcome to the club. Either way, Smithers followers continue to disappoint their middle school guidance counselors by still not living up to their potential.

The German psychiatrist Kurt Goldstein and other organismic theorists posited that the main purpose of humans, in fact their only true motive, is to "actualize" themselves, which is to reach their full potential in life. The American psychologist Abraham Maslow brought this concept to the mainstream with his hierarchy of needs theory. According to Maslow, after more basic physical and psychological needs are met, self-actualization, the highest level of personal development, can be achieved. He believed that the self-actualized individual, as a requisite for achieving all they are capable of, must be "independent of the good opinion of others."

Smithers followers turn this notion on its head. They are the opposite of independent of the good opinion of others. They live for the approval of others; especially their leaders. I'm not saying that there is anything wrong with staying in your boss's good graces. That's how you keep your job. I am saying that harboring a desperate desire for their approval is no way to live, man. Leaders recognize this and often take advantage of the situation.

Sounds a lot like a cult, right? David Arnott, in his book *Corporate Cults, The Insidious Lure of the All-Consuming Organization*, argues that workplaces can be cult-like. Just like with religious cults, workplaces can be all about the leaders and their whims, rules, approval, and favorites. Arnott calls out Microsoft as a cult because he believes its employees are cut off from the real world and are obsessed with achieving great things for Bill

Gates. That might be a bit of a stretch (nobody's drinking poisoned Kool-Aid because Windows 20 is clunky and crash prone), but he does have a point. Apple, for another, seems to encourage a cult-like devotion from its employees and consumers as part of its branding.

Rick Ross, the founder and executive director of The Cult Education Institute, has identified ten warning signs of an unsafe leader. How many of these apply to the folks at the top in your workplace? Eight or more yeahs and you just might be working for the next Jim Jones or Steve Jobs.

1. Absolute authoritarianism without meaningful accountability.
2. No tolerance for questions or critical inquiry.
3. No meaningful financial disclosure regarding the budget or their expenses.
4. Unreasonable fear of the outside world, such as impending catastrophe, evil conspiracies and persecutions.
5. There is no legitimate reason to leave. Former followers are always wrong for leaving.
6. Former members often relate the same stories of abuse and reflect a similar pattern of grievances.
7. There are books, news articles, or television programs that document the abuses of the group or leader.
8. Followers feel they can never be good enough.
9. The leader is always right.
10. The leader is the exclusive means of knowing truth or receiving validation.

A person typically doesn't start with the intention of being either a Smithers or a cult leader. But somehow, somewhere along the path, they end up that way. Jim Jones, founder of the People's Temple and the man responsible for the deaths of over 900 of his followers, first rose to prominence by promoting racial equality and helping the poor of Indianapolis. Fifteen years later, he was in the jungle in South America doling out cups of Flavor-Aid laced with cyanide. We know that power corrupts, so it's not all that surprising that an idealistic leader would stray- maybe not as far as Jim Jones did. But what about the followers here? What causes a person to become a Smithers, to join an organization because of a passion for racial equality but end up staying because of a passion for its leader? It could be transference.

Sigmund Freud formulated the concept of emotional transference, which he introduced in 1895 in his book *Studies on Hysteria,* after observing that a good number of his psychoanalysis patients, both men and women, developed an intense attachment to him, even love for him, in the course of their treatments. (What an ego Freud must have had. You'd think he'd invented it.) He realized that some other force must be at work here, because, frankly, he wasn't all that lovable. Freud came to the conclusion that his patients were transferring feelings from past relationships onto him. These relationships were often with a close family member, usually a parent, and from their childhood.

Transference has since become a well-documented phenomenon, and it's not just confined to the therapist-patient dynamic. It's common for all sorts of folks to project profound and powerful emotions from childhood onto anyone in their present lives, including their bosses. And the conscious mind has no idea that the subconscious is doing this. Yes, you do it, too. You're just not aware of it.

It happens in the workplace when you're introduced to the new guy on the crew, and he seems oddly familiar. Although your work buddies seem OK with him, there's just something about the guy that bugs you. One day on a jobsite, he questions your technique when you're cutting a two-by-four and you suddenly explode in rage. Your overreaction startles your coworkers who tell you they've never seen you act like this before. "It has been a long time," you think. "Not since I was a kid and my big brother would nitpick at me for everything." At that moment, it dawns on you who the new guy reminds you of, and that you just reenacted a scene that occurred thirty years ago in the basement of your parents' house. Transference has regressed you to a child at work. And the Department of Labor has strict rules about children in the workplace.

The boss-follower relationship, like the one between therapists and patients, is particularly susceptible to the transference dynamic. This is because bosses and parents share a lot of the same characteristics so it's natural to unknowingly project feelings from your childhood for a parent onto your current supervisor. (And you thought your work relationships weren't as complicated as your home ones. Ha!) This helps explain why boss-follower interactions can be so emotionally charged and messy. It also explains why feelings and experiences we had as children can still affect us as adults.

Psychologists say that maternal and paternal transference stems from our desire as children for safety and security amid a frightening world. As children, we have no control over the seemingly chaotic and unsettling environment called the universe which we found ourselves born into. One of the few countermeasures children can take is to endow a person close to them, like their mother or father, with the power to tame these uncertainties, and thus provide the child with order, comfort, safety, and security. Followers engaging in maternal or paternal transference endow their leaders with the same power for the same reasons. They're not necessarily looking for a substitute mommy or daddy, just someone who can soothe some of their workplace anxiety.

When maternal/paternal transference is added to the mix in the leader-follower relationship game, an already complicated dynamic becomes even more so- for both parties. Followers affected by positive transference view their leaders in an idealized way. They're less inclined to second guess their decisions and tend to have strong, impassioned loyalty to them. Positive transference is like an emotional Super Glue that binds followers to their leaders.

There are downsides to all this, of course. For one, powerful authority figures in our lives, even those we've bestowed with that power, can cause as much anxiety as they alleviate. For followers, a sense of dependence and submission tends to arise from the transference process, which unscrupulous leaders are quick to take advantage of. Plus there's the whole negative maternal/paternal transference thing, where followers project all the lousy qualities of their rotten parents onto their poor unsuspecting bosses. Transference is a big deal. For Freud, he thought his patients were ready to end their therapy only after they understood and could control their transference feelings.

Unless you work in a family-run business, your boss is not your mother and your boss is not your father. Harboring a subconscious belief that you'll be treated at work with the same amount of care and consideration that your parents provided will leave you in a perpetual state of disappointment. And you won't even understand why you're feeling that way. If you're not getting along with the boss or you're following a leader who's not worthy of you, it may be time to take an honest self-inventory. Until you can appreciate your relationships for what they really are, and not saddle them with your emotional baggage, you'll always be susceptible to transference.

Guinevere Turner, who spent the first ten years of her life as a member of The Fort Hill Community, never understood why her mother stayed with the cult for so long. Mel Lyman, the group's founder and leader, was the harmonica player for the legendary Jim Kweskin Jug Band. He infamously closed out the 1965 Newport Folk Festival, where Bob Dylan was first booed for going electric, with a 20-minute harmonica solo based on the old hymn Rock of Ages. Lyman taught his followers that the world was going to end on January 5, 1974, but that they would be saved by U.F.O.s, which would whisk them away to a new life on Venus.

When the world didn't end and the spaceships never materialized, Lyman told his followers it was all their fault. And they believed him. He said that their souls weren't ready for the trip. His was more than ready, but they hadn't put in the spiritual work necessary for such a journey. Lyman purportedly died in 1978, but the group is still around today, apparently still preparing their souls for that trip to Venus and operating a successful home remodeling business on the side. Really.

It was as a teenager that Turner asked her mother, "Did you really believe we were going to live on Venus?" (The planet has an average surface temperature of 860 degrees Fahrenheit.) "It's complicated," her mother said. "You can hold a lot of conflicting ideas at once sometimes. You'll understand when you're older." But Turner never could. It's hard for sane, rational people to comprehend that much lack of critical thinking.

Smithers-types and cult followers are very good at engaging in the willing suspension of disbelief. They can enjoy a book or movie despite its preposterous premise and plot holes you can drive a truck through. (That's not me, by the way.) When they're in the throes of the cult they may even begin to perceive themselves as a character in a work of fiction. These are people who seek drama, both real and imagined. They might be better served in their lives, however, if they took on the role of critic rather than method actor movie star.

The relationship between leader and effective follower is symbiotic, but it should also be one of conflict, of competing goals. For the boss, it makes good business sense to promote devotion to the organization and to himself personally. For employees, things can go horribly wrong if their devotion is based solely on the boss. Blind loyalty is not only a logical fallacy, but a tough way to earn a living, man.

Hollow followers are the most common type of follower in the workplace. These are the folks who are just going through the motions: people close to retirement who stopped caring a few years back or those who for whatever reason never cared beyond their paycheck in the first place. They're the guys in the matching jumpsuits and hardhats in the background of all those James Bond movies keeping the lair running for the evil genius villain. (How do you even apply for a job as an HVAC mechanic on Dr. No's island?) They don't seem particularly invested in world domination. If they were, it wouldn't always take half an army of them to capture Bond only to have him slip away.

The Urban Dictionary defines this syndrome well, which it calls "Short Timer's Disease." It's the inability to care about your job or your co-workers. Symptoms include coming in late, leaving early, not bothering to learn the names of new co-workers, not participating at meetings, and doing just enough to skate by. Short timers are disengaged. They've left the tribe in all but body.

I get it if you're a hollow follower and you're a year or two from retirement and a full pension. (Or if you've already secured a better job and are just playing out your two weeks' notice.) But what about those employees who are fifteen years from drawing a pension, yet have a full-blown case of short timer's disease. They perform their duties as a clerk at the permits counter in the county office building like they're serving a long prison sentence for a thought crime.

Many of them appear to be following the advice given to James Houston, a former inmate at San Quentin State Prison, by a fellow inmate when he first started his residency there: walk slowly and drink plenty of water. Houston said, "This basically means to pay close attention to your surroundings and don't do too much talking." (Which is sound advice for almost any circumstance.) People who are that miserable in their jobs should do the world a favor and move on. The inmates at San Quentin certainly would if they could.

While hollow followers are found everywhere, their most favored habitat seems to be federal, state and local government jobs. There's something about the nature of that work that turns ordinary townsfolk into the bureaucratic undead. It might be the combination of high job security and low job satisfaction. According to data from the Bureau of Labor Statistics, private sector employees are three times more likely to get fired than those working government jobs.

At one time, the flipside of all this job security was that government jobs tended to pay less than their counterparts in the private sector. But those days are gone. The Congressional Budget Office has concluded that Federales are overpaid. The CBO reported that on average federal salaries and benefits are 17 percent higher than private-sector levels. While that's not exactly golden handcuffs, it certainly qualifies as silver home detention ankle bracelets. And they bind hollow followers to jobs that they should have left years ago.

Job burnout is also a major cause of hollow followership. In 2019, the World Health Organization's *International Statistical Classification of Diseases and Related Health Problems* updated its entry on job burnout. It's now defined as a "syndrome conceptualized as resulting from chronic workplace stress that has not been successfully managed." Huh? With all due respect to the WHO, that definition appears to be the work of a sloppy, lazy, burned out bureaucrat or an automated random phrase generator. Either way, it doesn't improve on the WHO's previous definition, which is almost poetically Zen-like in its simplicity. Burnout: a state of vital exhaustion.

Rome didn't fall in a day and you don't get to a state of vital exhaustion overnight. Experts say that job burnout happens gradually. Passionate, motivated, highly productive employees over time become disillusioned, disengaged, cynical, indolent followers. That's right. You can't be suffering from burnout if you were never highly motivated in the first place. Burnout is the domain of fallen overachievers and former go-getters.

Don't let them tell you it's all your fault either. Research has shown that the work environment and the leader contribute greatly to increasing the likelihood of this syndrome. According to the Harvard Business Review, "People are most likely to experience burnout in the face of conditions such as unrealistically high workloads, low levels of job control, incivility, bullying, administrative hassles, low social support, poor organizational resources, stressed leaders, and negative leadership behaviors." Where leaders are toxic, followers burn out.

It seems almost cruel to tell a person suffering from vital exhaustion to "rediscover your passion," but that's the common advice given to the terminally burned out. Not that it's bad advice. It's just not very helpful. (A more useful bromide for them might be "fake it until you make it.")

The remedy for job burnout is complicated by the fact that it requires action where one of the major indicators of vital exhaustion is inaction. Vital exhaustion is characterized by excessive fatigue, increasing irritability, and feelings of demoralization, but its affects actually cut straight to the heart. Literally. Research suggests that vital exhaustion can exert its pathophysiological influence on cardiovascular disease. Your job *can* give you a heart attack- in spite of all the time you've spent at your standing desk reading the company's wellness newsletter.

What is the role of passion in overcoming or preventing job burnout? Overrated buzzword or essential fundamental? I think it depends a lot on the job. Some jobs, especially those that don't pay well and directly serve at-risk populations such as children and the elderly require a lot of passion to make it through the day. They are demanding jobs that beseech your passion. If you've become a special educator for any other reason (the fortune or fame maybe?) than a love of helping special learners, vital exhaustion is inevitable. Other jobs, not so much.

It depends a lot on the passion, too. Not all passions are created equal. Many psychologists subscribe to the dualistic model of passion, which helps explain why sometimes passion can prevent job burnout and other times exacerbate it. In this model there are two types of passion: harmonious and obsessive. Both can facilitate feelings of engagement and motivation in the workplace. The difference is that people control harmonious passions; obsessive passions control them.

When people enthusiastically take on work projects that are aligned with their self-identity and values, but still feel they can duck out at five some evenings to attend their daughter's softball games, they are experiencing harmonious passion. This sense of choice coupled with gratification and identity alignment are the hallmarks of this passion. Harmonious passion, as you surmised, is a positive driving force in the follower's life.

But sometimes people are compelled to undertake a work activity for the wrong reasons, such as the promise of recognition, reward, approval, or acceptance. The activity may be something they don't enjoy doing or even something that goes against their personal beliefs. If they don't perform it well or complete it, these individuals may experience feelings of guilt and diminished self-esteem. These feelings can be powerful, motivating forces, but they're not nurturing. They don't sustain you. Guilt and self-loathing will only take you so far. Vital exhaustion is inevitable.

Two Followers' Tales

LION: "What makes the Hottentot so hot? What puts the 'ape' in apricot? What have they got that I ain't got?"

ME: "Courage."

Stanislav Yevgrafovich Petrov was born and raised near the city of Vladivostok, in the far eastern region of Russia. The city is Russia's largest port on the Pacific and home to the nation's Pacific Fleet. Petrov's father was a military man, having served as a fighter pilot during World War II; his mother worked as a nurse. He went to college in Kiev, nearly 4,500 miles due west of his home, and, like his father, joined the Soviet Air Force. He rose quickly through their ranks, eventually becoming a lieutenant colonel assigned to the early-warning systems for the Soviet Air Defense Forces.

It was in a command center bunker outside of Moscow in the early morning hours of September 26, 1983, that Petrov, as the 44-year-old officer on duty, quite possibly saved the world. His job was to monitor the satellite systems and notify his superiors when they indicated that a nuclear missile attack against the Soviet Union was imminent. The strategy when such an attack was detected was for the Soviet Union to launch an immediate, full-scale nuclear counter-attack against the U.S. This strategy was quite literally

MAD (Mutually Assured Destruction), a military doctrine and national security policy adopted by both sides to ensure the total destruction of the attacker, counter-attacker, and a whole lot of other folks in the event of a nuclear war.

In 1983 relations between the U.S. and U.S.S.R. were frosty. The Soviets believed that the U.S. was clandestinely preparing for a nuclear first strike against them. Leonid Brezhnev, General Secretary of the Communist Party, and Yuri Andropov, KGB chairman, declared their belief of this to the country's leadership in 1981. President Ronald Reagan, in a March 8, 1983 speech to the National Association of Evangelicals, famously referred to the Soviets as the "evil empire" and "the focus of evil in the modern world." On September 1, the Soviet military shot down a South Korean passenger jet that had inadvertently strayed into its airspace, killing all 269 people aboard including a U.S. Congressman. The Soviets were fully expecting a reprisal. And on September 26th that's just what it appeared they were getting.

Their early-warning system detected an intercontinental ballistic missile from the United States heading its way. "The siren howled, but I just sat there for a few seconds, staring at the big, back-lit, red screen with the word 'launch' on it," Petrov said in a 2017 interview. "There was no rule about how long we were allowed to think before we reported a strike, but we knew that every second of procrastination took away valuable time, that the Soviet Union's military and political leadership needed to be informed without delay. All I had to do was to reach for the phone; to raise the direct line to our top commanders."

But he didn't. He couldn't. Petrov's intuition and training guided his decision making. Petrov believed that had it been an actual first strike by the U.S., the system would have detected more than just a lone missile. He suspected that the launch detection system was malfunctioning, though he had no way of confirming this other than waiting to see if a nuclear warhead would actually explode over Russia - which is what he decided to do. "Twenty-three minutes later I realized that nothing had happened. If there had been a real strike, then I would already know about it. It was such a relief," he said.

Later that day, the system warned of four additional missiles from the U.S. headed towards the Soviet Union, a warning that Petrov also ignored. It was determined later that these false alarms occurred because satellites misread sunlight reflecting off high-altitude clouds as incoming missiles. Experts believe that had Soviet leadership been informed that the early warning systems detected missiles from the U.S., their most likely reaction would have been to launch a counter strike. Petrov's followership undoubtedly saved the lives of hundreds of millions of people.

And what became of Petrov? Was he presented with the Order of Lenin for his insightful inactions that day? Not exactly. A short time after the incident, Petrov received an official reprimand. It wasn't for failing to immediately report that incoming missiles were about to strike the Soviet Union. In true bureaucratic lunacy, it was because he didn't fill out his logbooks correctly for that day. He told leaders that he was a little preoccupied at the time with things besides logbooks, but it didn't matter. Petrov left the military the following year, and he lived most of his life in quiet obscurity, his story only coming to light after the collapse of the Soviet Union.

Janet (not her real name) moved from her hometown of Butler, Pennsylvania, a small city in the western part of the state, to Indianapolis six months prior to take a job with a large manufacturer of construction materials - doors, windows, siding, roofing shingles, etc. It was a big move for her. She was a single mother with a twelve-year-old son in tow. Janet hadn't lived outside of Western Pennsylvania before and didn't know anyone in Indiana, but the opportunity was just too good to pass up. She was in charge of client and employee product education, a role she was well suited for, having performed the same duties for eight years at another manufacturer before it moved its operations to Mexico. "Indianapolis has got to be better than Matamoros," she thought.

And for the first three months or so, Janet was right. She loved her new job. Her coworkers were friendly and supportive. Linda, her boss, seemed to be appreciative of the knowledge and experience she brought to the position.

The two of them joked about the Colts/Steelers rivalry and where to find the best pierogis in town. All was good, and then it wasn't.

It started small. Linda cut her off abruptly at one of the weekly staff meetings when Janet was talking about a situation at her old company. It gradually grew to outright contempt. Linda would roll her eyes or look down or shake her head in disapproval nearly every time Janet spoke at meetings. Janet brushed it off at first by focusing on the positive. She still enjoyed the work and others in the company seemed to appreciate her contributions to the team. "What does it matter if the boss is a jerk?" she thought. But it did matter. Janet resisted the urge to confide in one of her coworkers about Linda. She was still the newbie and wasn't sure who she could trust. Besides, there was a part of her that couldn't quite believe what was happening and thought that she might be overreacting.

Then on a large teleconference meeting which included Linda, Linda's boss, Janet and a dozen other employees in the division, all Janet's doubts were dispelled. In a discussion about the rollout of a new line of residential windows, Linda interjected sarcastically, "I'm sure Janet will have something to say about it. She has something to say about everything else around here." There was an awkward silence for a few moments before the discussion returned to the marketing plan. No one followed up on Linda's remarks. Janet dared not speak up. She felt humiliated, and worse, she felt that the other people on the call were embarrassed for her.

She actually did have strong opinions about the rollout, particularly regarding the strategy of marketing the windows directly to consumers rather than to businesses. This was the first time the manufacturer had ventured from the B2B model, and Janet's experience and intuition led her to believe they were setting themselves up for a big flop. They risked losing their long-standing relationships with their most important customers (retailers, contractors and remodeling businesses) to enter a world of direct-to-consumer marketing they were not prepared for. Janet had given it some thought and developed a plan on how to better differentiate the marketing strategies to both groups without alienating their core customer base.

The next morning, she stopped by Linda's office and asked if she had a few minutes to speak with her. Linda motioned her in, and Janet entered, closing the door behind her. "There're some potential pitfalls in the rollout of the new windows that haven't been addressed, and I've identified some strategies for how to deal with them," Janet said, handing Linda a two page document detailing her concerns and proposed solutions. Linda thanked her and said she would review the plan and get back to Janet with her comments.

"Oh, and one more thing. I'd like to transfer," Janet told her. "There's an opening in logistics, and I was wondering if you'd put in a word for me with the manager over there." Linda was genuinely surprised. When she asked Janet why she wanted out, Janet plainly, clearly, and stoically recounted instances in her present job when she felt she was treated disrespectfully, culminating with Linda's comments at the teleconference the previous afternoon.

Linda didn't exactly apologize or acknowledge that she'd done anything wrong. "I'm sorry that you feel that way," she said. "I certainly didn't mean to make you feel disrespected. But I can see how you could." Linda then spoke briefly about why a transfer wouldn't be in Janet's best interests before turning the conversation back to the new product line. She thanked Janet again for her analysis of the rollout plan and promised they would meet again soon to go over it. As Janet was getting up to leave, Linda said to her, "And I want to thank you for speaking to me today about how you feel."

Janet and Linda never became BFFs, but their working relationship improved dramatically from that point onward. Many of Janet's ideas were incorporated into the rollout strategy for the new windows, which proved to be a success. Linda went so far as to acknowledge Janet's contributions on the project at one of her staff meetings. There was still plenty of room for improvement in the work environment, but at least Janet had hope for the future.

About eighteen months later, their paths crossed in the parking lot of a medical supply company across town. Janet was walking back to her car after interviewing for the marketing manager position there when she looked up and caught Linda's eye as she was headed toward the building for her own interview. They acknowledged each other with a quick, knowing smile, but neither ever mentioned it or got the job. Linda left the company about six months later. Janet applied for her position, and although she didn't get the job, found herself working closely with Linda's replacement, who valued, trusted, and supported her. And that's all Janet ever wanted, to be part of a team.

It would appear at first blush that these followers and their situations could not be more different. For one, the lives of hundreds of millions of people, maybe even the fate of the entire world, hung in the balance. For the other, it was a new line of single hung windows. But I wouldn't say that one situation was any more stressful than the other. If I were forced to choose, I would argue that Janet's predicament was more fraught with pressure than Petrov's. If Petrov were wrong, so what? He would be dead, his bosses would be dead, his bosses' bosses would be dead, and the United States would be crowned winner of the cold war. La-di-da.

But if Janet didn't play her cards right, she probably would have had to uproot her entire life again and the life of her young son and move back home with her folks, where the chances of finding another job in her field were slim. She probably would have had to take some drag job just for the health benefits and could have found herself stuck there for many, many years. Don't talk to me about nuclear Armageddon. Being a single parent and living in your parents' basement in Western Pennsylvania and working as a receptionist at the local cannabis dispensary- now that should send chills down anyone's spine. (No offense to my weed loving friends in the Keystone State.)

What Janet and Petrov have in common, with each other and with all the most effective followers, is, in a word, courage. Courage is a mindset and the single most important prerequisite for effective followership. It's a decision to take the best course of action despite your fears and nagging insecurities, vulnerabilities, flaws and self-proclaimed inadequacies. This is opposed to bravery, which is a trait that doesn't involve conscious decision making. Courage must be cultivated. Bravery is something you're born with.

When asked, brave people will often say that they never considered the danger- they just jumped in with no regard for their own safety. As a wag once said, "The only difference between bravery and stupidity is the outcome." The etymology of the words is telling. Bravery comes from the Italian word "bravo," which means "bold" but also once meant "savage." Courage draws from the French word "cuer", meaning "heart."

"Courage" and "heart" are not typically words associated with followership, but they ought to be. It's going to take plenty of both to navigate the path of effective followership. Hell, it's going to take plenty of both just to start on the path. But what would we be if we didn't even try?

About the Author

Geoff is a proud human resources professional with over thirty years of experience in compensation management, recruitment and staffing, and position classification. He lives in Timonium, Maryland with his wife, Mary Alice, and two spoiled house cats. *Followership: A Practical Guide to Surviving Leaders* is the culmination of years of research and reflection on the topic. Geoff is available to share his wealth of experience and knowledge of this emerging management field with audiences everywhere. To learn more visit followership.work.